A GIFT FOR:

....

FROM:

....

DATE:

....

JACK COUNTRYMAN

THE POWER OF
HOPE

100
DEVOTIONS
*to Build
Your Faith*

COUNTRYMAN®

An Imprint of Thomas Nelson Publishers

THOMAS NELSON
Since 1798

The Power of Hope

© 2021 Jack Countryman

Published in Nashville, Tennessee, by Thomas Nelson. Thomas Nelson is a registered trademark of HarperCollins Christian Publishing, Inc.

Thomas Nelson titles may be purchased in bulk for educational, business, fundraising, or sales promotional use. For information, please email SpecialMarkets@ThomasNelson.com.

Unless otherwise noted, Scripture quotations are taken from the New King James Version®. Copyright © 1982 by Thomas Nelson. Used by permission. All rights reserved.

Scripture quotations marked AMP are from the Amplified® Bible (AMP). Copyright © 2015 by The Lockman Foundation. Used by permission. www. Lockman.org

Scripture quotations marked ESV are from the ESV® Bible (The Holy Bible, English Standard Version®). Copyright © 2001 by Crossway, a publishing ministry of Good News Publishers. Used by permission. All rights reserved.

Scripture quotations marked HCSB are from the Holman Christian Standard Bible®. Copyright © 1999, 2000, 2002, 2003, 2009 by Holman Bible Publishers. Used by permission. HCSB® is a federally registered trademark of Holman Bible Publishers.

ISBN 978-1-4002-2496-8 (HC)
ISBN 978-1-4002-2494-4 (eBook)
ISBN 978-1-4002-3379-3 (Audiobook)

Printed in China

21 22 23 24 25 GRI 10 9 8 7 6 5 4 3 2 1

CONTENTS

INTRODUCTION

Among the many gifts God pours into the lives of His children is hope. Some might even say God is in the business of hope. After all, He's been giving people hope since the days of Eden, when the about-to-be-exiled Adam and Eve desperately needed it.

Again and again in Scripture, we see God blessing His people with hope. For starters, Noah, Abraham, Joseph, Moses, David, Daniel, Mary, Paul, and many others. As we look at scenes from these people's lives, we see how God-given hope gave His people power, the kind of power only He can provide.

We can learn about living with hope and about the power of hope when we look at people whose stories are in the Bible. But let's not stop there. Before you read each passage, ask God to show you the lesson He wants you to both learn and apply in your own life. Ask His Spirit to help you know God better. As you do, you'll come to trust more completely the One who, because He is love, provides you with hope and the power of hope.

In its accounts of Jesus' crucifixion, the Bible paints

a clear picture of God's great love for us. We can rest in the Almighty's presence with absolute assurance that Jesus gave His life on the cross for us. What amazing love! May Jesus' ultimate sacrifice enable you to know with absolute certainty that you are truly loved by your heavenly Father. And may each of us go boldly to the throne of grace with a humble heart to receive the life-giving, strength-giving hope that only God can give.

Jack Countryman

LOVING GOD: OUR HIGHEST PRIORITY

As the deer pants for the water brooks,
So pants my soul for You, O God.
My soul thirsts for God, for the living God.
When shall I come and appear before God? . . .
Why are you cast down, O my soul?
And why are you disquieted within me?
Hope in God, for I shall yet praise Him
For the help of His countenance.
PSALM 42:1-2, 5

The Psalmist

What does God want most from us? He wants us to love Him. He created us to be in intimate relationship with Him. He made us to thirst for Him with the same intensity we have when, parched and dry, we seek water for our physical thirst.

Sometimes—like this psalmist—we don't even know why we feel dry, why we feel discouraged or sad. In those times we need to *choose* to put our hope in God, to draw on His strength, and to receive the grace He has for us. May we also remember that God loves us with an everlasting love, and He truly wants the best for us. He longs for us to go to Him regularly with our hearts open to receive His love, mercy, and grace.

When your relationship with God is your highest priority, you will know divine strength and unshakable hope.

2

HONORING OUR GOD

Blessed are You, LORD God of Israel,
our Father, forever and ever.
Yours, O LORD, is the greatness,
The power and the glory,
The victory and the majesty. . . .
In Your hand is power and might;
In Your hand it is to make great
And to give strength to all.
I CHRONICLES 29:10-12

David

King David wanted to build a house for his great, powerful, glorious God, but the Lord gave that privilege to David's son Solomon.

To honor God and help Solomon succeed, David gave his personal fortune—about 113 tons of gold and 214 tons of silver—to the building project. Then David invited the people to join him. They, too, gave willingly and generously: 188 tons of gold, 377 tons of silver, 679 tons of bronze, 3,775 tons of iron, and precious jewels (1 Chronicles 28–29 MSG). No wonder David responded with a song of praise!

The people had been generous. Perhaps they understood what we need to understand and remember: everything we have comes from God. We give nothing to God that He, our good Father, has not first given to us. Who wouldn't praise such a God?

Like the Israelites, may we worship God by joyfully, generously giving to His work in this world.

3

THE GREATEST POWER: LOVE

*Love suffers long and is kind; love does not envy;
love does not parade itself, is not puffed up; does
not behave rudely, does not seek its own, is not
provoked, thinks no evil; does not rejoice in iniquity,
but rejoices in the truth; bears all things, believes
all things, hopes all things, endures all things.*

*Love never fails. . . . Now abide faith, hope, love,
these three; but the greatest of these is love.*
I CORINTHIANS 13:4–8, 13

Paul

The author of these well-known 1 Corinthians 13 verses is the apostle Paul. On a murderous mission to destroy Jesus-followers, Paul himself became a follower (Acts 9). He had witnessed Stephen's stoning, "made havoc of the church" (Acts 8:3), and then set off to Damascus to continue his persecution of believers—yet later he wrote 1 Corinthians 13. Apparently those Jesus-followers Paul had once persecuted taught him a lot about Christian love.

God *is* love. The gift of His Son to die on the cross for our sins reveals His love. When we pray and He says, "Not yet," we can trust in His love. When people disappoint and tragedies occur, we can trust in His love. When we face difficult decisions, we can depend on His guiding love. When God's love is our dwelling place, we live with hope, finding strength for the day and abundant love to share.

4

THE POWER OF THE HOLY SPIRIT WITHIN

*If there is no resurrection of the dead, then Christ is not risen.
And if Christ is not risen, then our preaching is empty and
your faith is also empty. . . . If Christ is not risen, your faith
is futile; you are still in your sins! . . . If in this life only we
have hope in Christ, we are of all men the most pitiable.*
I CORINTHIANS 15:13-14, 17, 19

Paul

Read today's scripture again and try to hear the words as if for the first time.

Simply put, there is no Christianity without the physical resurrection of Jesus from the dead. Christian persecutor turned Jesus-follower, the apostle Paul knew this critical truth as the *gospel*, meaning "good news." The hope we have in Christ rests on the fact that He—surrendering His life—made the ultimate sacrifice for our sins on the cross, rose from the tomb on the third day, and is alive today.

Do you realize, though, that "the Spirit of Him who raised Jesus from the dead dwells in you" (Romans 8:11)? His Spirit leads us, empowers us, and fuels our hope. The Spirit of the risen Christ provides us with God's strength, direction, peace, and, yes, hope.

Christ is risen! He is risen indeed!

5

THE HOPE GOD'S CHILDREN HAVE

*I, John, saw the holy city, New Jerusalem, coming down
out of heaven from God, prepared as a bride adorned
for her husband. And I heard a loud voice from heaven
saying, "Behold, the tabernacle of God is with men. . . .
And God will wipe away every tear from their eyes;
there shall be no more death, nor sorrow, nor crying."*

REVELATION 21:2–4

John

John was a disciple of Jesus, one of the Twelve. He and his brother James were Zebedee's sons, but the Lord had nicknamed them *Sons of Thunder*. Perhaps they earned that name when a Samaritan village refused to accept Jesus, and the two offered to call down fire in response (Luke 9:54)! Toward the end of his life, John—exiled to the island of Patmos—wrote the book of Revelation.

Definitely a unique genre, Revelation offers great hope to believers. We may not fully understand all that's going on with the censers, trumpets, and dragon, but we do find hope in statements like "There shall be no more death, nor sorrow, nor crying" (Revelation 21:4). Now, *that* is hope!

6

A LESSON IN GRACE

*Gird up the loins of your mind, be sober, and rest
your hope fully upon the grace that is to be brought
to you at the revelation of Jesus Christ*
1 PETER 1:13

Peter

Peter knew about grace—and the lesson had been painful.

Confident Peter claimed he would die with Jesus—until a servant girl accused him of being with the recently arrested Jesus of Nazareth. Peter denied knowing Jesus two more times before—exactly as Jesus had prophesied—a rooster crowed. After making eye contact with Jesus, Peter left the courtyard, weeping bitterly. The risen Lord, though, extended His disciple abundant grace—the grace of forgiveness, the grace of once again calling Peter to "Follow Me" (John 21:19).

Like Peter, we will disappoint our Lord—and ourselves—when we do something we know He doesn't want us to do or we don't do something we know He wants us to do. Peter's experience gives us hope for those times: Jesus will extend to us the grace of forgiveness. The hope of that grace gives us strength to get up when we fall.

7

THE MESSAGE OF REDEMPTION AND HOPE

You were not redeemed with corruptible things,
like silver or gold . . . but with the precious blood of
Christ, as of a lamb without blemish and without
spot. . . . [He] was manifest in these last times for
you . . . so that your faith and hope are in God.
1 PETER 1:18–21

Peter

In the preceding devotion, we saw Peter at perhaps his lowest moment: to save himself, Peter denied knowing Jesus. Today we see Spirit-filled, Spirit-empowered Peter preaching the message of our redemption by "the precious blood of Christ":

> Jesus of Nazareth, a Man attested by God to you by miracles, wonders, and signs . . . being delivered by the determined purpose and foreknowledge of God, you have taken by lawless hands, have crucified, and put to death; whom God raised up, having loosed the pains of death, because it was not possible that He should be held by it. (Acts 2:22–24)

We are to follow Peter's example and share the news of Jesus. When was the last time you shared the gospel and told someone what Jesus means to you? The Lord is glorified when you tell others about His love, mercy, and grace. In addition, your faith is strengthened and your hope renewed.

8

A LIVING HOPE

Blessed be the God and Father of our Lord Jesus Christ, who according to His abundant mercy has begotten us again to a living hope through the resurrection of Jesus Christ from the dead, to an inheritance incorruptible and undefiled and that does not fade away, reserved in heaven for you.

I PETER 1:3-4

Peter

Our God is a faithful Promise Maker and Promise Keeper: He always faithfully keeps the promises He makes to us less-than-faithful human beings.

Imagine being Peter. Imagine the guilt, the heartache, perhaps even the shame that this disciple experienced after he disappointed his Lord—and himself—by denying that he even knew the Man. Later, forgiven and once again following Jesus, Peter went on to know imprisonment, controversy, and martyrdom, reportedly—at his request—being crucified head down because he wasn't worthy of being crucified in the exact same way his Lord had been.

Like Peter, you and I do not have a dead Savior; we have a living hope. Peter knew this truth, and his letters testify to his faith and his hope. The resurrection of Jesus guarantees that God will always keep His promises to His children. That hope keeps us going in the darkest of times.

9

THE HOPE OF CHRIST'S RETURN

*The Lord Himself will descend from heaven with a shout, with
the voice of an archangel, and with the trumpet of God. And
the dead in Christ will rise first. Then we who are alive and
remain shall be caught up together with them in the clouds
to meet the Lord in the air. And thus we shall always be with
the Lord. Therefore comfort one another with these words.*
I THESSALONIANS 4:16-18

Paul

Knowing that waiting for Jesus' return would be difficult, the apostle Paul wrote to encourage believers—then and now—to hope in our Lord and Savior's return. Not wanting his brothers and sisters in Thessalonica to "sorrow as others who have no hope" (1 Thessalonians 4:13), Paul offered some specifics about the moment the Lord returns for His church, specifics perhaps revealed to him when he "was caught up to the third heaven" (2 Corinthians 12:2).

First, "the dead in Christ will rise" (1 Thessalonians 4:16). Next, people who are alive will "be caught up together . . . in the clouds to meet the Lord in the air" (v. 17). Then—the best news and greatest hope of all— "We shall always be with the Lord" (v. 17). What a glorious truth to fuel our hope!

May our lives reflect the hope we have in Jesus and the promise of His return.

10

STEADFAST HOPE

*We give thanks to God always for you all, making
mention of you in our prayers, remembering
without ceasing your work of faith, labor of love,
and patience of hope in our Lord Jesus Christ.*
I THESSALONIANS 1:2-3

Paul

But hadn't he tried to destroy the new church? And now he was preaching the gospel?

Yes and yes. Paul had—literally—seen the light of God's truth, committed his life to the risen Lord, and served his God as church founder, pastor, teacher, and writer. Along the way Paul was imprisoned, scourged, beaten, stoned, shipwrecked, and in peril (2 Corinthians 11:23–28). Yet he remained strong in his faith, encouraging believers in the churches he founded and us today.

In today's passage, Paul commended believers for "patience of hope," translated elsewhere as "steadfastness of hope" (ESV), "endurance of hope" (HCSB), and in the Amplified Bible, "your work energized by faith, and your service motivated by love and unwavering hope in [the return of] our Lord Jesus Christ."

As Jesus promised, a life of faith will involve suffering. Paul suffered—but his hope in Jesus Christ held strong. Will yours?

GOD'S PROMISE TO ABRAHAM

"Get out of your country,
From your family
And from your father's house,
To a land that I will show you.
I will make you a great nation;
I will bless you
And make your name great;
And you shall be a blessing.
I will bless those who bless you,
And I will curse him who curses you;
And in you all the families of the earth shall be blessed."

GENESIS 12:1-3

Abraham

I t was a remarkable act of obedience. Abram—whom we know as Abraham—heard God say, "Get out of your country . . . [Go] to a land that I will show you," and Abram did exactly that.

Along the way, God repeated His covenant promises to Abraham—promises of descendants, a great name, land, blessings, and the opportunity to bless others. God's covenant with Abraham offered him an unwavering source of hope, something Abraham needed when his faith wavered.

After twenty-five years of waiting for the first of the promised descendants who would someday be as numerous "as the stars of the heaven" (Genesis 22:17), one-hundred-year-old Abraham and ninety-year-old Sarah welcomed Isaac into this world.

When our faith wavers, let's open God's Word, read about His faithfulness to Abraham, and review His promises to us, His children. May we, like Abraham, live with hope because of the promises of God.

12

HOPING IN GOD'S PROVISION

*The LORD God caused a deep sleep to fall on Adam, and he
slept; and He took one of his ribs, and closed up the flesh in
its place. Then the rib which the LORD God had taken from
man He made into a woman, and He brought her to the man.
And Adam said:
"This is now bone of my bones
And flesh of my flesh;
She shall be called Woman,
Because she was taken out of Man."*
GENESIS 2:21-23

Adam

The first task that God gave Adam, the first man, was naming every beast and bird that He had created. "But," the Genesis account sadly reports, "for Adam there was not found a helper comparable to him" (2:20). Yet it seems that God got to work right away to remedy that situation. Hear the joy of Adam's words when God brought him Eve: "This is now bone of my bones."

Now consider the hope we can find in today's scripture. God saw a need in Adam: companionship. God met that need: Eve. Adam received God's gift with joy. How amazing and wonderful to be known so well, provided for so completely, and loved so deeply by almighty God!

Just as God responded to Adam's hope—to his need—for a companion, God responds to His people's hopes and needs today, for our good and for His glory.

13

HOPING IN WHOM?

The anger of the Lord was kindled against Moses, and He said: "Is not Aaron the Levite your brother? I know that he can speak well. And look, he is also coming out to meet you. . . . Now you shall speak to him and put the words in his mouth. And I will be with your mouth and with his mouth, and I will teach you what you shall do. So he shall be your spokesman to the people. And he himself shall be as a mouth for you, and you shall be to him as God."

EXODUS 4:14-16

Aaron

Three times Moses had objected to being Israel's spokesman and going before Pharaoh. Neither the burning-but-not-burning-up bush, nor the rod-turned-snake-turned-rod, nor the clean-hand-turned-leprous-made-clean hand, nor God's promise to be with him had convinced Moses that he could do whatever God called him to do. Despite all his conversations with God, Moses still doubted his ability to speak to Pharaoh on the Lord's behalf. No wonder God was angry!

So God called Aaron to be the spokesman for Israel, and Moses would be the intermediary, speaking on God's behalf and telling Aaron what to say.

Before we judge Moses, remember that God has called us to share the hope of the gospel with people who have not yet heard it. Are you willing, as Aaron was—or do you object, as Moses did?

In other words, when you respond to Jesus' Great Commission, who or what are you hoping will help you?

14

GROWING IN FAITH AND HOPE

Ananias answered, "Lord, I have heard from many about this man, how much harm he has done to Your saints in Jerusalem."...

But the Lord said to him, "Go, for [Saul] is a chosen vessel of Mine to bear My name before Gentiles, kings, and the children of Israel."...

Ananias went his way and entered the house; and laying his hands on [Saul] he said, "Brother Saul, the Lord Jesus, who appeared to you on the road as you came, has sent me that you may receive your sight and be filled with the Holy Spirit."

ACTS 9:13, 15-17

Ananias

I t was a strange, even dangerous assignment.
God called Ananias, a follower of Jesus, to go to Saul
(later named Paul)—the zealous persecutor of Jesus-
followers—who had lost his ability to see when the
resurrected Jesus appeared to him and transformed this
persecutor into a preacher.

Without his confidence that he had heard God's
voice and without his hope that God would protect
him and enable him to obey, Ananias would never have
answered the Lord's call. But doing as the Lord had commanded, Ananias found Paul exactly where God had
said. Similarly—and exactly as God had revealed to Paul
in a vision—a man named Ananias arrived, he put his
hand on Paul, and this new disciple could once again see.

Because Ananias obeyed, both he and Paul undoubtedly grew in faith and in hope. What is God asking you to
do that would grow your faith and hope?

15

FEAR OR HOPE?

Joshua the son of Nun and Caleb the son of Jephunneh,
who were among those who had spied out the land, tore
their clothes; and they spoke to all the congregation
of the children of Israel, saying: "The land we passed
through to spy out is an exceedingly good land. . . . Do
not rebel against the LORD, nor fear the people of the
land. . . . The LORD is with us. Do not fear them."

NUMBERS 14:6–7, 9

Joshua and Caleb

Joshua and Caleb were in the minority. The report of the other ten men God had sent to spy out the land of Canaan was very different from Joshua and Caleb's. Those ten brought back not only a cluster of grapes that required two men to carry it on a pole, but also stories of giants in the land, stories that filled the people of God with fear.

But Joshua and Caleb stood up and said, "The land we passed through to spy out is an exceedingly good land," yet the people didn't listen.

Joshua then reminded them that the Lord would help them take the land. But the people had lost hope; they no longer trusted the Lord.

When our hope wavers, let's look at the cross. There we see immeasurable love, promises made and kept, resurrection power, and a reason to hope, whatever our circumstances.

16

HOPING IN THE HOLY SPIRIT'S WORK

Now the Lord is the Spirit; and where the Spirit of the Lord is, there is liberty. But we all, with unveiled face, beholding as in a mirror the glory of the Lord, are being transformed into the same image from glory to glory, just as by the Spirit of the Lord.
2 CORINTHIANS 3:17–18

Paul

Paul's conversion experience was dramatic. This one-time persecutor of Jesus' early followers went on to write thirteen New Testament letters about theology, living out our faith in Christ, and honoring God with our lives—and we're still reading those letters today.

We're also going through the same process of becoming more like Jesus (*sanctification* is the fancy word) that people in the first-century church—and every century since—went through. When we first recognize Jesus as our Savior and receive forgiveness for our sin, the Holy Spirit comes to dwell inside us and begin His work in our hearts and minds. As the Spirit molds us into the image of Jesus, we are "being transformed into [His] same image from glory to glory." What an amazing truth!

And what a solid source of hope! The Holy Spirit will help us become the people God created us to be!

17

SHARING OUR HOPE

*About the ninth hour of the day [Cornelius]
saw clearly in a vision an angel of God coming
in and saying to him, "Cornelius!"*

*And when he observed him, he was afraid,
and said, "What is it, lord?"*

*So he said to him, "Your prayers and your alms have
come up for a memorial before God. Now send men
to Joppa, and send for Simon whose surname is Peter.
He is lodging with Simon, a tanner, whose house is
by the sea. He will tell you what you must do."*
ACTS 10:3-6

Cornelius

———————————

Cornelius was a Roman soldier who walked with God. When the Lord's angel gave Cornelius instructions, Cornelius obeyed.

While the angel visited Cornelius, the Lord was preparing Peter—a Jew—to accept the radical invitation to enter a Gentile's home. Placing his hope and trust in God, Peter went with Cornelius's emissaries. When he arrived at Cornelius's home and saw a gathering of family and friends, Peter preached the gospel, the good news of hope in God, hope for today and hope for eternity.

This Jew and this Gentile faithfully obeyed God's instructions and moved boldly in an unprecedented, perhaps uncomfortable direction. God has also instructed us to move in a not necessarily comfortable direction: we are to share the gospel—the good news of forgiveness of sin and of eternal life—with friends, acquaintances, and family. This week, whom will you tell about the difference Jesus has made in your life?

18

LIVING OUT OUR FAITH AND HOPE

Blessed be the name of God forever and ever,
For wisdom and might are His. . . .
He gives wisdom to the wise
And knowledge to those who have understanding.
He reveals deep and secret things;
He knows what is in the darkness,
And light dwells with Him.
I thank You and praise You,
O God of my fathers;
You have given me wisdom and might,
And have now made known to me what we asked of You,
For You have made known to us the king's demand.

DANIEL 2:20-23

Daniel

An exile in Babylon after the siege in Jerusalem, Daniel remained committed to the Lord. He remained faithful in his prayer life, his eating habits, and his worship. Day in and day out, Daniel walked closely with his God.

When King Nebuchadnezzar learned that Daniel was gifted in understanding visions, he called for the young Hebrew. When Daniel was able to tell Nebuchadnezzar not only what his dream was but also its meaning, Daniel praised the Lord with a song that includes the lines in today's passage. Later, standing in front of the king, Daniel gave God all the credit and all the glory (Daniel 2:28).

Let us follow Daniel's example and be faithful in our prayer life, our worship, and our Bible study. Let us also be faithful to give God the glory when He uses us and faithful to share the gospel of hope when He gives us the opportunity.

19

MAKING BIG REQUESTS OF OUR BIG GOD

Elijah said to Elisha, "Ask! What may I do for you, before I am taken away from you?"

Elisha said, "Please let a double portion of your spirit be upon me."

So he said, "You have asked a hard thing. Nevertheless, if you see me when I am taken from you, it shall be so for you; but if not, it shall not be so." Then it happened, as they continued on and talked, that suddenly a chariot of fire appeared with horses of fire, and separated the two of them; and Elijah went up by a whirlwind into heaven.
2 KINGS 2:9-11

Elijah

E lijah had passed the prophetic baton to Elisha and would soon be taken to heaven by the God he had walked with throughout his life. Aware of the magnitude of the position he was assuming, Elisha asked to receive "a double portion of [Elijah's] spirit." Elisha made this big request because he had come to know a great God, and our great God responded in a big way.

What big things might God be pleased to do in your life if you would only ask Him? Knowing that God wants to use you for His glory, what big thing might you ask for regarding your ministry at home, at work, at church, or wherever God has you? The Lord is pleased when we walk with Him, surrender our lives to His will, and place our hope in Him.

And He hears and responds to His people's big prayers.

HOPING IN OUR SOVEREIGN GOD

Esther was taken to King Ahasuerus, into his royal palace, in the tenth month, which is the month of Tebeth, in the seventh year of his reign. The king loved Esther more than all the other women, and she obtained grace and favor in his sight more than all the virgins; so he set the royal crown upon her head and made her queen.

ESTHER 2:16-17

Esther

G od often demonstrates His grace to His children by giving us not only unexpected blessings but also unexpected power or influence. Whenever the latter happens, it is no accident. That power or influence is the plan of our sovereign God.

It was, for instance, His sovereign hand that placed Esther on the throne in Persia, a position that gave Esther an opportunity to live out in a bold way the strength she found when she placed her hope in God. Queen Esther risked her life by going—uninvited—before the king to arrange a time when she could ask him to prevent the genocide of her Jewish people. God showed her grace and favor when He prompted the king to show her grace and favor. And as He did for Esther, God will do for you whenever you boldly live out your hope in your sovereign God.

21

GROWING HOPE

Gideon said to God, "If You will save Israel by my hand as You have said—look, I shall put a fleece of wool on the threshing floor; if there is dew on the fleece only, and it is dry on all the ground, then I shall know that You will save Israel by my hand, as You have said." And it was so. . . . Then Gideon said to God, "Do not be angry with me, but let me speak just once more: Let me test, I pray, just once more with the fleece; let it now be dry only on the fleece, but on all the ground let there be dew." And God did so that night. It was dry on the fleece only, but there was dew on all the ground.

JUDGES 6:36-40

Gideon

As Gideon hid in a winepress to thresh his wheat—so his Midianite enemies wouldn't steal it—God called Gideon to destroy the altar of Baal and then to save Israel from the Midianites. Similar to reluctant Moses, Gideon said, "O my Lord, how can I save Israel?" (Judges 6:15). Clearly Gideon's doubts outweighed whatever hope he had in the Almighty. Hence the fleece.

God agreed to Gideon's test and delivered—twice! Whether from a lack of trust in God, a lack of courage, or both, Gideon clearly didn't want to lead Israel against the Midianites and Amalekites. But when he did, he saw that God was true to His promise "I will be with you" (v. 16).

The Lord may have a big assignment for you just as He had for Gideon. Know that stepping out—with God—to do battle will strengthen your faith and grow your hope.

22

A PRAYER OF HEARTFELT HOPE

*[Hannah] was in bitterness of soul, and prayed to the
Lord and wept in anguish. Then she made a vow and
said, "O Lord of hosts, if You will indeed look on the
affliction of Your maidservant and remember me, and not
forget Your maidservant, but will give Your maidservant
a male child, then I will give him to the Lord all the days
of his life, and no razor shall come upon his head."*
I SAMUEL 1:10-11

Hannah

She had undoubtedly watched relatives and friends have babies. Her husband's other wife had several sons and daughters—and lorded them over her barren rival. Oh, how Hannah longed for a baby of her own.

During one of the family's annual trips to the tabernacle, Hannah prayed to the Lord. Overcome by great anguish and that profound heartache she had known for far too long, she once again asked almighty God for a son. Out of profound gratitude should God give her a child, Hannah vowed to give him to the Lord. Her beloved son would live, work, and learn in the tabernacle.

Nine months later, Hannah bore a son—named Samuel—who grew up to be a prophet and judge over all of Israel.

Our gracious God granted Hannah the son she had prayed for with heartfelt hope and trust in the Lord. May we learn from her example.

23

THE SPIRIT OF GOD WITHIN YOU

"I will pray the Father, and He will give you another Helper, that He may abide with you forever—the Spirit of truth, whom the world cannot receive, because it neither sees Him nor knows Him; but you know Him, for He dwells with you and will be in you. . . .

"These things I have spoken to you while being present with you. But the Helper, the Holy Spirit, whom the Father will send in My name, He will teach you all things, and bring to your remembrance all things that I said to you. . . .

"When He, the Spirit of truth, has come, He will guide you into all truth; for He will not speak on His own authority, but whatever He hears He will speak; and He will tell you things to come."
JOHN 14:16-17, 25-26; 16:13

The Holy Spirit

How well do you know the Holy Spirit? To get to know Him better, let's see what Jesus said about this fellow member of the Trinity.

The Holy Spirit will guide us into all truth about our God and our Savior. The Holy Spirit will also guide us in everyday life, in big decisions and in not-so-big ones. The Holy Spirit helps believers discern what is true and what is not; what is wise and what is foolish; what is the best and what is simply good.

As our Guide rather than our master, the Holy Spirit will not force us to do anything. Whether to follow or not follow His leading remains our choice. That choice is easier when we remember that the One who shepherds us is our Helper, our Teacher, and the Spirit of truth. May we therefore unhesitatingly put our hope in the Spirit's guidance.

24

FAITHFUL TO THE FAITHLESS

The LORD said to me [Hosea], "Go again, love a woman who is loved by a lover and is committing adultery, just like the love of the LORD for the children of Israel, who look to other gods and love the raisin cakes of the pagans."

So I bought her for myself for fifteen shekels of silver, and one and one-half homers of barley. And I said to her, "You shall stay with me many days; you shall not play the harlot, nor shall you have a man—so, too, will I be toward you."

HOSEA 3:1-3

Hosea

I t's a love story. A one-sided love story . . .
God told the prophet Hosea to take the prostitute
Gomer as his wife. Faithful Hosea obeyed: he truly
loved her, consistently provided for her, and would have
welcomed a soul-to-soul relationship with her. Instead,
Gomer opted for a series of lovers who sought only their
own pleasure and offered her nothing but a few trinkets.

Before judging Gomer, though, let's acknowledge
that we commit her same sins every time we turn from
loving God and instead run after something else: a big-
ger house, a better job, an exciting relationship. The
children of Israel had the same tendency. May we do
what faithless Israel eventually did: "return and seek the
Lord their God. . . . They shall fear the Lord and His
goodness in the latter days" (Hosea 3:5).

Hear this hope: our faithful God waits for us unfaithful ones to return to Him.

25

AN ASSIGNMENT WITHOUT HOPE

Abraham took the wood of the burnt offering and laid it on Isaac his son; and he took the fire in his hand, and a knife, and the two of them went together. But Isaac spoke to Abraham his father and said, "My father!"

And he said, "Here I am, my son."

Then he said, "Look, the fire and the wood, but where is the lamb for a burnt offering?"

And Abraham said, "My son, God will provide for Himself the lamb for a burnt offering."
GENESIS 22:6-8

Abraham

"T ake now your son . . . and offer him there as a burnt offering" (Genesis 22:2). That was God's chilling command to Abraham . . . and he obeyed.

What was Abraham thinking on the journey to Moriah? *Did I hear God right? Why would He ask me to do this? Maybe He'll change His mind. This seems out of character, so different from the God I know.* Did any hope exist in his breaking heart as he prepared to take his son's life?

What was Isaac thinking? *I don't understand what Abba is doing. We need a lamb. This makes no sense.* Isaac wouldn't have dreamed he was to be the sacrifice.

When Abraham lifted the knife to kill his son, the angel of the Lord called, "Abraham, Abraham!"—and provided a ram for the offering (vv. 11–13).

God spared Abraham's son but not His own. Jesus' death and resurrection mean forgiveness of sin, eternal life, and hope that the Lord will always provide.

26

A LIFE-CHANGING ENCOUNTER

In the year that King Uzziah died, I saw the Lord sitting on a throne, high and lifted up, and the train of His robe filled the temple. Above it stood seraphim; each one had six wings: with two he covered his face, with two he covered his feet, and with two he flew. And one cried to another and said:
"Holy, holy, holy is the Lord of hosts;
The whole earth is full of His glory!"

And the posts of the door were shaken by the voice of him who cried out, and the house was filled with smoke.
ISAIAH 6:1-4

Isaiah

I saiah's life changed dramatically when he saw the Lord seated on His heavenly throne. This breathtaking vision of God pierced Isaiah to his very core, and the prophet cried out, "I am a man of unclean lips, and I dwell in the midst of a people of unclean lips; for my eyes have seen the King, the Lord of hosts" (Isaiah 6:5).

We will never deal effectively with our sin without realizing—as Isaiah did—who God is in all His glory and holiness. A clearer understanding of God's sinlessness prompts humility before Him and reverence in our relationship with Him.

Like Isaiah, you and I fall short of God's perfect holiness, yet find hope in the fact that God loves you deeply. He will equip you for whatever He calls you to do. He will be present with you always. Let's not hesitate to place our hope in Him.

27

WRESTLING WITH THE DIVINE

*Jacob was left alone; and a Man wrestled with him until
the breaking of day. Now when He saw that He did not
prevail against him, He touched the socket of his hip; and
the socket of Jacob's hip was out of joint as He wrestled
with him. And He said, "Let Me go, for the day breaks."*

But he said, "I will not let You go unless You bless me!"

So He said to him, "What is your name?"

He said, "Jacob."

*And He said, "Your name shall no longer be called
Jacob, but Israel; for you have struggled with
God and with men, and have prevailed."*
GENESIS 32:24-28

Jacob

At the place of Jabbok, "Jacob was left alone," but he wasn't alone for long.

During the night Jacob suddenly found himself in a wrestling match that lasted until daybreak. Jacob's hip was put out of joint as he struggled with this mysterious stranger, but Jacob refused to release his grip until he received a blessing.

Jacob's struggle prompted the One he had wrestled to change his name to *Israel*, meaning—appropriately—both "Struggle with God" and "Prince with God." In response, Jacob named the spot of the wrestling match *Peniel,* "for I have seen God face to face, and my life is preserved" (v. 30).

Jacob undoubtedly never forgot this experience, one that surely fueled his hope in almighty God wherever he was, whatever he faced.

Find hope in knowing that God—who is the same yesterday, today, and forever—is also with you wherever you are, whatever you face.

28

"FOLLOW ME"

*As [Jesus] walked by the Sea of Galilee, He saw Simon
and Andrew his brother casting a net into the sea; for
they were fishermen. Then Jesus said to them, "Follow
Me, and I will make you become fishers of men." They
immediately left their nets and followed Him.*

*When He had gone a little farther from there, He saw
James the son of Zebedee, and John his brother, who also
were in the boat mending their nets. And immediately
He called them, and they left their father Zebedee in the
boat with the hired servants, and went after Him.*

MARK 1:16-20

Four Fishermen

What kind of person could compel someone's allegiance with two simple words? What kind of personality could prompt men to leave behind their livelihood and accept the invitation?

Simon, Andrew, James, and John were fishermen. Hardy and hardworking, physically strong, probably rough-edged and gruff as a result of working in this man's world. Yet when Jesus said, "Follow Me," they did.

The fishermen may have heard about this Rabbi's teaching. Luke is the only gospel writer reporting that before calling these four disciples, Jesus had cast out unclean spirits and healed people, Peter's mother-in-law among them. Maybe the news had gotten around.

Or maybe Jesus, eye-to-eye and face-to-face, is not someone you easily say no to. Winsome, gentle, strong, warm, captivating, intriguing, authoritative—God Incarnate would be all this and so much more.

Will you follow Him into a life of purpose and service, of joy and hope?

29

"IT IS WRITTEN . . ."

Jesus was led up by the Spirit into the wilderness to be tempted by the devil. And when He had fasted forty days and forty nights, afterward He was hungry. Now when the tempter came to Him, he said, "If You are the Son of God, command that these stones become bread."

But He answered and said, "It is written, 'Man shall not live by bread alone, but by every word that proceeds from the mouth of God.'" . . .

Then the devil left Him, and behold, angels came and ministered to Him.
MATTHEW 4:1–4, 11

Jesus Christ

Satan challenged Jesus two more times, and Jesus again responded to those temptations with truth from God's Word. Scripture teaches not to test God, so Jesus wasn't going to leap from the height of the temple, and Scripture teaches to worship only God, so He would not bow down before Satan.

Did you notice verse 1, though? *The Spirit* led Jesus "into the wilderness to be tempted by the devil"! We should never doubt God's leading just because we run into temptation. That can be God's way of strengthening and growing our faith.

And did you notice Satan's strategy? He will urge us to think that God can't be trusted or hasn't spoken the entire truth. Like Jesus, may we respond to temptations by appealing to the Word of God: "It is written . . ." We can hope in the power of Scripture to enable us to stand against temptation.

30

SPEAKING HOPE

Then the LORD said to Satan, "Have you considered My servant Job, that there is none like him on the earth, a blameless and upright man, one who fears God and shuns evil?"...

So Satan went out from the presence of the LORD, and struck Job with painful boils from the sole of his foot to the crown of his head. And he took for himself a potsherd with which to scrape himself while he sat in the midst of the ashes.

Then his wife said to him, "Do you still hold fast to your integrity? Curse God and die!"

But he said to her, "You speak as one of the foolish women speaks. Shall we indeed accept good from God, and shall we not accept adversity?"

JOB 2:3, 7–10

Job

Life is hard, dark times come, and so do seasons of hopelessness.

After God gave Satan permission to test Job, this faithful man experienced the excruciating loss of family, servants, flocks, herds, and buildings. Then came the boils that covered his body. And Job's response is a model for us: "Shall we indeed accept good from God, and shall we not accept adversity?"

When we face difficult circumstances, let's choose to continue to believe that the Lord is with us. Hope and faith are a believer's best responses in times of hardship and trial, and those responses require an exercise of the will. At times we must say aloud to ourselves, "I know God has a purpose in this. I know God will bring me through this."

If no one speaks hope to you, you need to speak it to yourself.

31

LOVING IN DEED

Whoever does not practice righteousness is not of God, nor is he who does not love his brother. For this is the message that you heard from the beginning, that we should love one another. . . .

By this we know love, because [Jesus] laid down His life for us. And we also ought to lay down our lives for the brethren. But whoever has this world's goods, and sees his brother in need, and shuts up his heart from him, how does the love of God abide in him?

My little children, let us not love in word or in tongue, but in deed and in truth.

1 JOHN 3:10-11, 16-18

John

O nce we accept Jesus as our Savior, God's Holy Spirit lives in us and enables us to serve as our Lord asks—and Jesus had a big ask for the apostle John. From the cross Jesus told John, "Behold your mother!" and we read, "From that hour that disciple took [Jesus' mother, Mary] to his own home" (John 19:27).

This same John, the author of today's passage, didn't just tell people to love "in deed"; he didn't just say we "ought to lay down our lives for the brethren." John did both. Welcoming Mary into his home surely impacted every aspect of his household: John had another mouth to feed, someone else to provide for, his Lord's own mother to care for until she died.

Yet God's people are to love one another. When we do so, people are blessed, and the world takes notice. May we love in deed!

32

A HERALD OF HOPE

*"You yourselves bear me witness, that I said, 'I am
not the Christ,' but, 'I have been sent before Him.' He
who has the bride is the bridegroom; but the friend of
the bridegroom, who stands and hears him, rejoices
greatly because of the bridegroom's voice. Therefore this
joy of mine is fulfilled. He must increase, but I must
decrease. He who comes from above is above all."*
JOHN 3:28-31

John the Baptist

John the Baptist was no doubt as rugged as the desert itself, a compelling no-holds-barred and mince-no-words preacher who attracted large crowds. This "voice of one crying in the wilderness" was calling people to repent and then baptizing them in the Jordan River after they confessed their sins (Mark 1:3).

John criticized the people for assuming they were righteous because they were the children of Abraham. He warned that they—despite their Jewish lineage—would be rejected unless they demonstrated fruits of repentance.

With this teaching and baptizing, John was preparing Israel for the coming Lord. Knowing the role God had called him to, John rejoiced in Christ's coming, understanding that "He must increase, but I must decrease." John was a forerunner of this mightier One, a herald of the messianic hope.

May we—with our actions as well as our words—be heralds of the hope we have in Jesus.

33

FLEEING FROM GOD'S PRESENCE

The word of the LORD came to Jonah the son of Amittai,
saying, "Arise, go to Nineveh, that great city, and cry out
against it; for their wickedness has come up before Me."
But Jonah arose to flee to Tarshish from the presence of
the LORD. He went down to Joppa, and found a ship going
to Tarshish; so he paid the fare, and went down into it, to
go with them to Tarshish from the presence of the LORD.
JONAH 1:1-3

Jonah

irst, a brief geography lesson:

F Jonah's hometown was Gath-Hepher, located in Galilee.

Nineveh—in Assyria (modern-day Iraq)—was more than five hundred miles northeast of Jonah's home.

Tarshish—Jonah's remote destination—was twenty-two hundred miles away in the exact opposite direction from Nineveh. Tarshish was on the southwest corner of Spain, on the other side of the Mediterranean from the seaport of Joppa.

Now read again Jonah 1:1–3. Do you understand more clearly Jonah's decision and actions?

Jonah was on the run, apparently forgetting what King David knew so well: "Where can I go from Your Spirit? Or where can I flee from Your presence?" (Psalm 139:7). The answer, of course, is nowhere.

May we not even *want* to escape God's presence. May we instead choose to serve Him, honor Him with our lives, and cling to the hope He offers. Let's not run away from Jesus, but toward Him.

34

OUR ONLY SOURCE OF HOPE

I know the thoughts that I think toward you, says the LORD,
thoughts of peace and not of evil, to give you a future and a
hope. Then you will call upon Me and go and pray to Me, and
I will listen to you. And you will seek Me and find Me, when
you search for Me with all your heart. I will be found by you,
says the LORD, and I will bring you back from your captivity.
JEREMIAH 29:11-14

Jeremiah

When have you been tempted to give up on a workout routine or an eating plan? On putting together that bucket-list trip, on pursuing a long-held educational goal, or maybe even on life itself? Discouragement is one of Satan's favorite weapons. Disappointments are inevitable, but we don't need to choose to respond with discouragement.

Recognizing how disheartened His people were while they were exiled in Babylon, God directed Jeremiah to speak words of hope and encouragement to them, to tell them that He had for them "a future and a hope."

When we're discouraged, let's remind ourselves of that truth. Let's also remember a theme communicated throughout God's Word: He is for us, not against us, and He always has our best in mind. God will use our disappointments and hardships for our benefit. He will also teach us to see Him as our only sure source of salvation, blessing, and hope.

35

FUEL FOR HOPE

The LORD was with Joseph, and he was a successful man;
and he was in the house of his master the Egyptian. And
his master saw that the LORD was with [Joseph] and that
the LORD made all he did to prosper in his hand. So Joseph
found favor in his [master's] sight, and served him. Then he
made [Joseph] overseer of his house, and all that he had he
put under [Joseph's] authority. So . . . the LORD blessed the
Egyptian's house for Joseph's sake; and the blessing of the
LORD was on all that he had in the house and in the field.

GENESIS 39:2–5

Joseph

I f you don't know Joseph's story, do a quick read of Genesis 37. The background will make today's passage more remarkable.

Of course Joseph didn't want to be sold into slavery by his own brothers and carried off to a new land. Yet, even when Joseph became the property of a powerful Egyptian official, the Lord was with him, blessing him as well as the official's house and fields.

Joseph was not at all where he wanted to be or had ever imagined being—and maybe that's true for you today. Perhaps Joseph wondered, *Is God not hearing my prayers? Has God forgotten me?* Those may be your questions too. Yet, in those far-from-ideal circumstances, God blessed Joseph's work in his master's house. Those blessings undoubtedly fueled Joseph's hope that God would one day change his circumstances.

As Joseph did, cling to the hope you have in God.

36

BOLDLY WITNESSING TO THE LORD OF HOPE

*When evening had come, because it was the Preparation
Day, that is, the day before the Sabbath, Joseph of Arimathea,
a prominent council member, who was himself waiting
for the kingdom of God, coming and taking courage, went
in to Pilate and asked for the body of Jesus. . . . [Pilate]
granted the body to Joseph. Then he bought fine linen,
took Him down, and wrapped Him in the linen. And
he laid Him in a tomb which had been hewn out of the
rock, and rolled a stone against the door of the tomb.*

MARK 15:42–43, 45–46

Joseph of Arimathea

I n Jesus' day, the Sanhedrin was the ultimate authority over Jewish religious, legal, and judicial matters, respected—perhaps feared—by the Jews they led. Joseph of Arimathea was a member of the Sanhedrin who, on the night Jesus was killed, boldly became public about his faith in Jesus. Going before Pilate, Joseph requested the body of Jesus and gave his Lord a rushed but decent burial. At Jesus' arrest, His closest disciples had run for their lives. In contrast, Joseph stepped forward, apparently unconcerned that revealing his allegiance to Jesus could cost him his reputation and more.

When have you been public about your faith? Do people in your neighborhood or workplace know you are a Jesus-follower, or are you basically a secret disciple, like Joseph of Arimathea? What is keeping you from being a bolder witness for Jesus and the love, joy, and hope He has for people?

37

"THE LORD IS WITH US"

Joshua the son of Nun and Caleb the son of Jephunneh, who were among those who had spied out the land, tore their clothes; and they spoke to all the congregation of the children of Israel, saying: "The land we passed through to spy out is an exceedingly good land. If the LORD delights in us, then He will bring us into this land and give it to us, 'a land which flows with milk and honey.' Only do not rebel against the LORD, nor fear the people of the land, for they are our bread; their protection has departed from them, and the LORD is with us. Do not fear them."

NUMBERS 14:6-9

Joshua

Twelve men, one from each tribe of Israel, entered the promised land to check out the terrain, the people, and the cities. After forty days, these men returned and declared that the land was indeed filled with milk and honey—but the people were huge and strong, and the cities were fortified.

Only two spies—Joshua and Caleb—spoke up, saying that the Lord would go before them and with them. The ten fear-filled spies won over the people, and the Lord's judgment followed: the people of Israel would wander in the wilderness for forty years (Numbers 14:34).

Because of their faith, God later allowed Joshua and Caleb to enter the promised land. Every other Israelite who lived at the time of the spying died without ever entering the land.

Are you and I—like Joshua and Caleb—willing to do big things for God because we know Him and hope in Him?

38

RESURRECTION HOPE

Jesus, again groaning in Himself, came to the tomb. It was a cave, and a stone lay against it. Jesus said, "Take away the stone." . . . Then they took away the stone from the place where the dead man was lying. . . . [Jesus] cried with a loud voice, "Lazarus, come forth!" And he who had died came out bound hand and foot with graveclothes, and his face was wrapped with a cloth. Jesus said to them, "Loose him, and let him go."

JOHN 11:38-39, 41, 43-44

Lazarus

Twice in his gospel the apostle John noted Jesus' love for Lazarus (11:5, 36), yet upon hearing of His friend's illness, Jesus waited two more days before going to Lazarus.

When Jesus finally arrived, both of Lazarus's sisters—Martha and Mary—made clear their displeasure with Jesus' timing: "If You had been here, my brother would not have died" (vv. 21, 32). The sisters had hoped Jesus would come immediately and heal their brother. Knowing Jesus loved Lazarus, they were saddened and puzzled by Jesus' late arrival. Their hope in Him seemed dashed—until they took Jesus to the tomb, and He brought Lazarus back to life.

Their hope had not been misplaced after all, and now their hope was renewed.

Let's learn from the sisters to hope in the Lord—whatever our circumstances—knowing that Jesus will validate our hope in Him in His way and in His timing.

39

HOPE DURING THE STORM

When evening had come, [Jesus] said to [His disciples],
"Let us cross over to the other side." Now when they had
left the multitude, they took Him along in the boat as He
was. And other little boats were also with Him. And a
great windstorm arose, and the waves beat into the boat,
so that it was already filling. But He was in the stern,
asleep on a pillow. And they awoke Him and said to Him,
"Teacher, do You not care that we are perishing?"

Then He arose and rebuked the wind, and
said to the sea, "Peace, be still!" And the wind
ceased and there was a great calm.
MARK 4:35–39

Jesus Christ

Think for a minute about the storms of life—a failed business, divorce, financial hardships, disease, needy parents, challenging teens, and the list goes on—that you've experienced. You may even be in a stormy time right now.

When a storm arises, do you respond, "God, I trust You to bring me through this"? Or do you tend to say, "I'm doomed! There's nothing anyone can do"?

One time, as Jesus and His disciples sailed across the Sea of Galilee, a terrible storm threatened their boat. The disciples panicked, woke up the napping Jesus, and asked, "Teacher, do You not care that we are perishing?" (How many times have you asked Jesus that question?)

When storms rage and fear rises, rely on the faith and hope God has given you. Exercise your faith in God: remember He is in control. Place your hope in God: know His peace.

40

REMEMBERING GOD'S FAITHFULNESS

*An Angel of the Lord appeared to [Moses] in a flame of fire
in a bush, in the wilderness of Mount Sinai. When Moses
saw it, he marveled at the sight; and as he drew near to
observe, the voice of the Lord came to him, saying, "I am
the God of your fathers—the God of Abraham, the God of
Isaac, and the God of Jacob." And Moses trembled and dared
not look. Then the Lord said to him, "Take your sandals
off your feet, for the place where you stand is holy ground.
I have surely seen the oppression of My people who are in
Egypt; I have heard their groaning and have come down to
deliver them. And now come, I will send you to Egypt."*

ACTS 7:30–34

Moses

The life of Moses was unique:

- His mother saved baby Moses' life by hiding him in a papyrus basket.
- The daughter of Pharaoh found the baby, so Moses was raised as royalty.
- Moses killed an Egyptian who had beaten a Hebrew slave—and Moses fled to Midian, where he stayed for forty years.

Then came God's dramatic call to Moses to perform a major—in fact, impossible—assignment: Moses was to return to Egypt, command Pharaoh to let God's enslaved people go free, and then lead his fellow Hebrews out of the land. Perhaps memories of the papyrus basket, life in Pharaoh's house, and the burning bush reminded Moses of God's faithfulness and strengthened his hope when traveling the wilderness got tough and God's people were grumbling.

You too will grow in faith and hope as you remember specific evidence of your faithful God's work in your life.

41

A WISE FRIEND'S COUNSEL

The LORD sent Nathan to David. And he came to him, and said to him: "There were two men in one city, one rich and the other poor. The rich man had exceedingly many flocks and herds. But the poor man had nothing, except one little ewe lamb which he had bought and nourished. . . . A traveler came to the rich man, who refused to take from his own flock . . . to prepare one for the wayfaring man . . . but he took the poor man's lamb and prepared it for the man who had come to him."

So David's anger was greatly aroused against the man. . . .

Then Nathan said to David, "You are the man! . . . You have killed Uriah the Hittite with the sword; you have taken his wife to be your wife. . . . David said to Nathan, "I have sinned against the LORD."

2 SAMUEL 12:1-5, 7, 9, 13

Nathan

T hink about a time when God blessed you with wisdom and hope through the counsel of a godly friend. The Lord often uses other believers to strengthen us, encourage us, and even confront us about our sin. A courageous example of the latter, the prophet Nathan confronted King David about his adultery with Bathsheba and his murder of her husband.

Willing to be used as the Lord's messenger, Nathan trusted God to direct his steps, provide the words, and prepare David's heart. God did exactly that when Nathan approached David about his grievous sin. "I have sinned against the LORD," David realized.

When a brother or sister in the Lord confronts you about sin in your life, humbly listen, ask God to confirm the message, and then confess your sin. Know that God will forgive you just as He forgave David. The hope of His grace is a sure thing.

42

HOPE AND POWER FOR THE TASK

[Nehemiah] said: "I pray, LORD God of heaven . . . please let
Your ear be attentive . . . that You may hear the prayer of
Your servant which I pray before You now, day and night, for
the children of Israel Your servants, and confess the sins of
the children of Israel which we have sinned against You. . . .
[We] have not kept the commandments, the statutes, nor
the ordinances which You commanded Your servant Moses.
Remember, I pray, the word that You commanded Your
servant Moses, saying, 'If you are unfaithful, I will scatter
you among the nations; but if you return to Me, and keep My
commandments . . . yet I will gather them.' . . . O Lord, I pray,
please let Your ear be attentive to the prayer of Your servant."
NEHEMIAH 1:5–9, 11

Nehemiah

Nehemiah's grief was profound: he had learned that the wall around his beloved Jerusalem had been destroyed. He wept, mourned, fasted, and prayed. First praising his God, Nehemiah then confessed that the people of Israel had broken God's law and sinned against Him. Then, reminding God of His promise to gather His repentant people, Nehemiah asked for that blessing as well as God's blessing on his conversation with King Artaxerxes, whom he served as cupbearer.

Nehemiah did receive permission from Artaxerxes to go to Judah to rebuild the Jerusalem wall. As he prepared, traveled, and did the construction work, Nehemiah depended on God for protection and guidance. He remained steadfast in his mission and strong in the hope of accomplishing the task God had placed on his heart.

Whatever task God has placed on your heart, find in the Lord, as Nehemiah did, hope and power to get it done.

43

STRENGTH FOR THE STRUGGLE

The good that I will to do, I do not do; but the
evil I will not to do, that I practice. . . .

I find then a law, that evil is present with me, the one who
wills to do good. For I delight in the law of God according
to the inward man. But I see another law in my members,
warring against the law of my mind, and bringing me
into captivity to the law of sin which is in my members. O
wretched man that I am! Who will deliver me from this body
of death? I thank God—through Jesus Christ our Lord!
ROMANS 7:19, 21-25

Paul

Paul knew—and preached, taught, and wrote about—the gospel: "If you confess with your mouth the Lord Jesus and believe in your heart that God has raised Him from the dead, you will be saved" (Romans 10:9). Jesus died to take the punishment for our sins, and He rose from the dead victorious over sin and death. Our belief in these truths means salvation from the eternal consequences of our sin.

Yet each of us knows the battle Paul described: we do what we don't want to do, and we don't do what we want to do. Just as we have trusted God to forgive us, we can trust Him—by the power of His Spirit in us—to give us strength for the struggle Paul described.

Who will deliver us from the power of sin in our life? Jesus Christ, our Lord, our Strength, our Hope.

44

TRUSTING GOD TO PROVIDE

I have learned in whatever state I am, to be content. . . .
Everywhere and in all things I have learned both to be
full and to be hungry, both to abound and to suffer need.
I can do all things through Christ who strengthens me.

Nevertheless you have done well that you shared in my
distress. . . . No church shared with me concerning giving
and receiving but you only. For even in Thessalonica you
sent aid once and again for my necessities. . . . Indeed I have
all and abound. I am full. . . . And my God shall supply all
your need according to His riches in glory by Christ Jesus.
PHILIPPIANS 4:11-16, 18-19

Paul

Jesus is the Author and Sustainer of life. He keeps our lungs breathing and our hearts beating. He provides necessary tangibles (food, water) and intangibles (wisdom, guidance). We truly can do nothing without Jesus.

Paul pointed out another thing we can't do without Jesus: we can't be content without Him. Life's demands can overwhelm us, but they are no match for the joy of the Lord and His peace that passes understanding.

When have you tried to meet your needs all by yourself—and realized you can't succeed? Know that God wants us in that position. Our loving and compassionate God does not delight in seeing our suffering or lack. But He does want us to acknowledge that He is the One who supplies all our needs, sometimes through His people, just as the Philippians provided for Paul.

And waiting for God to provide strengthens our faith in Him.

45

LIVING OUT HOPE IN GOD

Noah found grace in the eyes of the LORD. . . . *Noah was a just man, perfect in his generations. Noah walked with God. . . . The earth also was corrupt before God, and the earth was filled with violence. . . .*

God said to Noah, "The end of all flesh has come before Me, for the earth is filled with violence through them; and behold, I will destroy them with the earth. Make yourself an ark of gopherwood. . . . I Myself am bringing floodwaters on the earth, to destroy from under heaven all flesh in which is the breath of life; everything that is on the earth shall die. But I will establish My covenant with you; and you shall go into the ark—you, your sons, your wife, and your sons' wives with you."

GENESIS 6:8-9, 11, 13-14, 17-18

Noah

Noah was saved by grace, an act of divine sovereignty. We too are saved by grace in an act of divine sovereignty. God called Noah and told him how to stay safe in the coming flood: build an ark. God calls us and invites us to stay safe from eternal separation from God: accept Jesus as our Savior and Lord.

Noah responded to God's call with obedience: he built the ark—one and a half football fields long—to save his family. Such human responsibility and divine sovereignty are not mutually exclusive. Noah walked with God, obeyed Him, and experienced the power that came with placing his hope in the Lord.

Do you respond to God with obedience, whatever He calls you to do? Once you accept the task, you'll see that human responsibility and divine sovereignty are actually complementary. Obey God and know the power of placing your hope in Him.

46

LOOKING TO JESUS IN FAITH

Jesus lifted up His eyes, and seeing a great multitude coming toward Him, He said to Philip, "Where shall we buy bread, that these may eat?"...

Philip answered Him, "Two hundred denarii worth of bread is not sufficient for them, that every one of them may have a little."

One of His disciples, Andrew, Simon Peter's brother, said to Him, "There is a lad here who has five barley loaves and two small fish, but what are they among so many?"

Then Jesus said, "Make the people sit down."... So the men sat down, in number about five thousand. And Jesus took the loaves, and when He had given thanks He distributed them to the disciples, and the disciples to those sitting down; and likewise of the fish, as much as they wanted.

JOHN 6:5, 7–11

Philip

As Jesus sat with His disciples on a mountainside, He saw the great and probably hungry multitude coming toward Him. Recognizing this as a teachable and faith-strengthening moment, Jesus turned to Philip for suggestions on how to meet the need.

Making some quick calculations, Philip exclaimed that even the wages from two hundred days of work would not buy enough bread to provide even a little food for everyone. It's curious that Andrew knew about—and then mentioned—five barley loaves and two small fish in the young boy's sack lunch. And Philip, Andrew, and the others were undoubtedly puzzled by Jesus' instructions to get the people seated. Their puzzlement turned to amazement as Jesus fed the several thousand people with the boy's meager lunch.

When you're not sure how to solve a problem, look to Jesus in faith, put your hope in Him, and watch what He does.

47

HOPING IN GOD, KNOWING HIS GRACE

The people shouted when the priests blew the trumpets.
And it happened when the people heard the sound of the
trumpet, and the people shouted with a great shout, that
the wall [of Jericho] fell down flat. Then the people went
up into the city. . . . And they utterly destroyed all that
was in the city, both man and woman, young and old,
ox and sheep and donkey, with the edge of the sword.

But Joshua had said to the two men who had spied out the
country, "Go into the harlot's house, and from there bring
out the woman and all that she has, as you swore to her."
JOSHUA 6:20-22

Rahab

Rahab's house was on the city wall of Jericho. She manufactured and dyed linen—and supplemented that income with prostitution. She contributed to Israel's conquest of Canaan when Joshua's two spies stayed at her house. Hiding them from the king's men, Rahab saved their lives.

Before letting the spies leave, Rahab told them what she knew about God: He had dried up the Red Sea and helped Israel destroy Sihon and Og, reports that had terrified the people of Jericho. Then she added her own statement of faith: "The Lord your God, He is God in heaven above and on earth beneath" (Joshua 2:11).

We don't know much about Rahab's journey to faith in God, but by His grace she had come to recognize His superiority over the idols of her culture. She had put her hope in Him and was saved.

Have you put your faith in "God in heaven above"?

48

A HARVEST FROM SEEDS OF HOPE

When [Naomi] saw that [Ruth] was determined
to go with her, she stopped speaking to her.

Now the two of them went until they came to
Bethlehem. And it happened, when they had come
to Bethlehem, that all the city was excited because
of them; and the women said, "Is this Naomi?"

But she said to them, "Do not call me Naomi; call me
Mara, for the Almighty has dealt very bitterly with me. I
went out full, and the LORD has brought me home again
empty. Why do you call me Naomi, since the LORD has
testified against me, and the Almighty has afflicted me?"
RUTH 1:18-21

Naomi

Looking around at the shambles of her life, Naomi saw only a barren field of sorrow. Her husband and both her sons had died, leaving her alone in Moab. But not completely alone. One of her daughters-in-law—Ruth—had declared her firm commitment to stay with Naomi and return with her to her hometown of Bethlehem.

Ruth's love was a sweet sign to Naomi that God had not abandoned her. As further evidence of God's hand on Naomi, He soon brought Ruth a husband and Naomi a grandson. God blessed Naomi with a rich and unexpected harvest of love.

Whatever situation you face, know that the Lord is with you and will sustain you. Keep reminding yourself of His great faithfulness to you; keep choosing to place your hope in Him. Like Naomi's, your barren field of sorrow will yield a rich harvest of God's blessings.

49

CONFIDENCE IN WHOM?

Samson said to the lad who held him by the hand, "Let me feel the pillars which support the temple, so that I can lean on them." Now the temple was full of men and women. All the lords of the Philistines were there—about three thousand men and women on the roof watching while Samson performed.

Then Samson called to the LORD, saying, "O Lord GOD, remember me, I pray! Strengthen me, I pray, just this once, O God, that I may with one blow take vengeance on the Philistines for my two eyes!" And Samson took hold of the two middle pillars which supported the temple. . . . And he pushed with all his might, and the temple fell on the lords and all the people who were in it. So the dead that [Samson] killed at his death were more than he had killed in his life.

JUDGES 16:26-30

Samson

God had blessed Samson with incredible strength, yet Samson never had the strength to conquer his weakness for pagan women. His downfall came with Delilah, who, at the prompting of Philistine lords, hounded Samson about the source of his great strength until he told her that his strength came from his hair. So the Philistines cut off his hair, and his strength disappeared along with God's favor. Led out from prison to entertain the Philistines, Samson experienced a brief return of divine strength, and he destroyed the temple and everyone in it, including himself.

Mighty in physical strength but weak in resisting temptation, Samson fell short of doing all he might have done for God. His hope in the Lord for his physical power had been slowly pushed aside by self-confidence and sinful disobedience.

Keep guard! Don't let your hope in the Lord become overconfidence and hope in yourself.

50

HOPE FULFILLED!

The LORD visited Sarah as He had said, and the LORD did for Sarah as He had spoken. For Sarah conceived and bore Abraham a son in his old age, at the set time of which God had spoken to him. And Abraham called the name of his son who was born to him—whom Sarah bore to him—Isaac. Then Abraham circumcised his son Isaac when he was eight days old, as God had commanded him. Now Abraham was one hundred years old when his son Isaac was born to him. . . . [Sarah] said, "Who would have said to Abraham that Sarah would nurse children? For I have borne him a son in his old age."
GENESIS 21:1-5, 7

Sarah

W hen God first promised countless descendants to Abraham, he and Sarah were living in Haran.

But ten years later—now seventy-five years old—Sarah remained barren. So, to help God fulfill His promise, and in accordance with the culture of the day, an impatient Sarah presented to Abraham her Egyptian maidservant, Hagar, with whom he could and did father a son named Ishmael.

Fifteen years later and far beyond childbearing age, ninety-year-old Sarah had given up hope of having a child of her own, yet she gave birth to Isaac. When God delivered this promised child, Sarah's hope in the Lord was restored.

God always keeps His promises, even to Sarah, whose story is—like yours and mine—one of both faith and the lack of faith, of both hope and the lack of hope. Despite her wavering faith and hope, God blessed Sarah, and He will bless you and me as well.

51

ASKING—AND RECEIVING

*"Now, O LORD my God, You have made Your servant
king instead of my father David, but I am a little child;
I do not know how to go out or come in. . . . Therefore
give to Your servant an understanding heart to judge
Your people, that I may discern between good and evil.
For who is able to judge this great people of Yours?"*

*The speech pleased the Lord, that Solomon had asked this
thing. Then God said to him: "Because you have . . . asked
for yourself understanding to discern justice, behold, I have
done according to your words; see, I have given you a wise
and understanding heart, so that there has not been anyone
like you before you, nor shall any like you arise after you."*

I KINGS 3:7, 9-12

Solomon

About twenty years old when he was crowned king, Solomon assumed the leadership of Israel at a time of great material and spiritual prosperity. Whether overwhelmed, humbled, or smart enough to know he didn't know everything, Solomon asked God for wisdom and discernment. Evidence that God gave Solomon wisdom comes next in 1 Kings 3.

When two women claimed to be the mother of the same baby, King Solomon spoke: "Divide the living child in two, and give half to one, and half to the other" (v. 25). Seeing the women's different reactions, Solomon declared that the one who would spare the child's life was clearly his mother.

Solomon asked God for wisdom, and James 1:5 invites us to do the same: "If any of you lacks wisdom, let him ask of God, who gives to all liberally and without reproach, and it will be given to him." Amen!

52

THE HOPE OF HEAVEN

When [the Sanhedrin] heard these things [Stephen
was saying,] they were cut to the heart, and they
gnashed at him with their teeth. But he, being full of
the Holy Spirit, gazed into heaven and saw the glory
of God, and Jesus standing at the right hand of God,
and said, "Look! I see the heavens opened and the
Son of Man standing at the right hand of God!"

Then they cried out with a loud voice, stopped their ears,
and ran at him with one accord; and they cast him out of the
city. . . . And they stoned Stephen as he was calling on God
and saying, "Lord Jesus, receive my spirit." Then he knelt
down and cried out with a loud voice, "Lord, do not charge
them with this sin." And when he had said this, he fell asleep.

ACTS 7:54–60

Stephen

What if you stood before a firing squad and the only way to avoid death was to deny your Lord?

Standing before the most powerful Jewish ruling body of the day, Stephen didn't back down from speaking the truth about his Lord. Stephen undoubtedly felt the leaders' anger intensify, and he knew that the penalty for speaking so-called blasphemy was stoning. Still, Stephen continued his overview of Israel's history: he had a point to make about the hardheartedness of the Sanhedrin.

Stephen wasn't intimidated by the Sanhedrin's wrath, because he had the hope of heaven. In fact, right before the Jewish leaders ran at him, Stephen looked to the heavens and saw his Lord. As he "fell asleep," Stephen's martyrdom beautifully displayed his faith in Jesus and his hope of eternal life with his Lord.

What aspects of your life reveal your faith in Jesus and your hope of eternal life with Him?

53

"UNLESS I SEE . . ."

After eight days [Jesus'] disciples were again inside, and
Thomas with them. Jesus came, the doors being shut,
and stood in the midst, and said, "Peace to you!" Then
He said to Thomas, "Reach your finger here, and look
at My hands; and reach your hand here, and put it
into My side. Do not be unbelieving, but believing."

And Thomas answered and said to
Him, "My Lord and my God!"

Jesus said to him, "Thomas, because you have
seen Me, you have believed. Blessed are those
who have not seen and yet have believed."
JOHN 20:26-29

Thomas

U nless I see in His hands the print of the nails, and put my finger into the print of the nails, and put my hand into His side, I will not believe" (John 20:25). Those were the words of Thomas, the disciple who had missed Jesus' first post-resurrection appearance to the disciples. Thomas wanted to see the Lord for himself.

Eight days later, Jesus again appeared to the disciples. Thomas was there, and his response? "My Lord and my God!"

Having doubted that Jesus had risen from the dead, Thomas had lost hope in his Lord. He had to see Jesus to believe and to again have hope for this life and eternal life. What did—or what will—it take for you to believe in Jesus, to receive His forgiveness, and to know hope in Him?

"Blessed are those who have not seen and yet have believed."

54

"BLESSED HOPE"

*The grace of God that brings salvation has appeared to all
men, teaching us that, denying ungodliness and worldly lusts,
we should live soberly, righteously, and godly in the present
age, looking for the blessed hope and glorious appearing of our
great God and Savior Jesus Christ, who gave Himself for us,
that He might redeem us from every lawless deed and purify
for Himself His own special people, zealous for good works.*

TITUS 2:11–14

God

Wat blessings of grace Paul outlines in this single—albeit long—sentence!

The apostle led with the grace of salvation, but God also teaches us both how to live a godly life and the truth that He redeems and purifies those of us who love Him. In addition, God calls us—and helps us—to be forward-looking, anticipating Jesus' glorious return as King of kings and drawing strength from the "blessed hope" of His second coming.

Life can be painful and disappointing, leaving us feeling beat-up and hopeless. Knowing that trials and tribulations come to His people, God encourages us through Paul's words to "[look] for the blessed hope." One day Jesus will come back in all His glory, victorious over sin and death, and "there shall be no more death, nor sorrow, nor crying. . . . no more pain" (Revelation 21:4). That truly is blessed hope.

55

HEARING GOD'S VOICE

The Lord called yet again, "Samuel!"

*So Samuel arose and [for the second time] went to Eli,
and said, "Here I am, for you called me." He answered,
"I did not call, my son; lie down again." . . .*

*And the Lord called Samuel again the third time. So he arose
and went to Eli, and said, "Here I am, for you did call me."*

Then Eli perceived that the Lord had called the boy.
I SAMUEL 3:6, 8

Samuel

Even one of the mightiest prophets of the Old Testament needed to learn how to hear God's voice and recognize it as such. That young prophet-to-be was named Samuel, and he served the Lord by serving the priest Eli.

Samuel was lying down one evening when Eli (who else would it be?) called his name, but Eli had not called Samuel. The third time this happened, Eli realized that the Lord was calling, so he instructed the boy to respond, "Speak, Lord, for Your servant hears" (v. 9).

Eli prompted Samuel to listen again to the voice—to God's voice. If we are going to be people of God who glorify our Lord as we serve Him, we also need to learn how to recognize His voice when He speaks to us. For starters, expect to hear God and know that whatever He says will never contradict His written Word.

56

A LIFE THAT COUNTS

There was a man named Zacchaeus who was a chief tax collector, and he was rich. And he sought to see who Jesus was, but could not because of the crowd, for he was of short stature. So he ran ahead and climbed up into a sycamore tree to see Him, for He was going to pass that way. And when Jesus came to the place, He looked up and saw him, and said to him, "Zacchaeus, make haste and come down, for today I must stay at your house." So he made haste and came down, and received Him joyfully.

LUKE 19:2-6

Zaccheus

You may know the story—and even the song—about this "wee little man" who "climbed up in a sycamore tree, for the Lord he wanted to see." It wasn't easy being one of the shortest and most hated men in the city, but the hatred was understandable. This Jewish tax collector worked for the Roman government and lined his pockets by overtaxing his fellow Jews. The crowd was horrified that Jesus had invited Himself over to that sinner's house!

Zaccheus had realized, though, that only by following Jesus would his life have purpose. Zaccheus's words to Jesus reveal his changed heart: "Look, Lord, I give half of my goods to the poor; and if I have taken anything from anyone by false accusation, I restore fourfold" (Luke 19:8).

Zaccheus had spent many lonely nights counting his money; now he wanted his life to count. Jesus will make your life count too.

57

SPREADING THE WORD OF THE LORD

Paul and Barnabas grew bold and said, "It was
necessary that the word of God should be spoken to
you first; but since you reject it, and judge yourselves
unworthy of everlasting life, behold, we turn to the
Gentiles. For so the Lord has commanded us:

'I have set you as a light to the Gentiles,
That you should be for salvation to the ends of the earth.'"

Now when the Gentiles heard this, they were glad
and glorified the word of the Lord. And as many
as had been appointed to eternal life believed.

And the word of the Lord was being
spread throughout all the region.
ACTS 13:46–49

Barnabas and Paul

A n apostle in the early church and Paul's companion
on his first missionary journey, Barnabas is perhaps
best known for being an encourager. (His name, in fact,
means "Son of Encouragement.") Case in point: when
Barnabas became a Christian, he sold his land and gave
the money to the Jerusalem apostles (Acts 4:36–37).

Shortly thereafter came the Holy Spirit's instruction:
"Now separate to Me Barnabas and [Paul] for the work
to which I have called them" (13:2). That work would
earn Paul the label "apostle to the Gentiles," take him on
four missionary journeys, and mean much persecution
(2 Corinthians 11:23–28). This first journey took Paul
and Barnabas from Antioch to Cyprus and through Asia
Minor before returning to Antioch.

What work has the Spirit called you to do? Who in
your path needs to hear the hope of the gospel? What a
privilege to spread the Word!

PASSING ON OUR HOPE

In the first year of his reign, in the first month, [King Hezekiah] opened the doors of the house of the LORD and repaired them. . . . [He] said to [the priests and the Levites]: "Hear me, Levites! Now sanctify yourselves, sanctify the house of the LORD God of your fathers, and carry out the rubbish from the holy place. For our fathers have trespassed and done evil in the eyes of the LORD our God; they have forsaken Him, have turned their faces away from the dwelling place of the LORD, and turned their backs on Him. . . .

"Now it is in my heart to make a covenant with the LORD God of Israel, that His fierce wrath may turn away from us."
2 CHRONICLES 29:3, 5-6, 10

Hezekiah

King Hezekiah "did what was right in the sight of the LORD, according to all that his father David had done" (2 Chronicles 29:2). Imagine having that said about you at the end of your life!

Yet Hezekiah's father did not earn such praise: Ahaz "did not do what was right in the sight of the LORD, as his father David had done" (28:1). Their great ancestor David—a man after God's own heart—pleased God. Ahaz, however, closed up the house of the Lord, preferring his Baals and child sacrifice (vv. 2–3). Then Hezekiah reopened the temple and called the priests and Levites back into service.

Think about your life. Are you more on Ahaz's path or Hezekiah's? What about your children and grandchildren, kids at church or in the neighborhood? What can you do to pass on to them the hope you have in Jesus?

59

REPENTANCE AND FORGIVENESS

Now it happened, as Jesus sat at the table in the house,
that behold, many tax collectors and sinners came and
sat down with Him and His disciples. And when the
Pharisees saw it, they said to His disciples, "Why does
your Teacher eat with tax collectors and sinners?"

When Jesus heard that, He said to them, "Those
who are well have no need of a physician, but those
who are sick. But go and learn what this means, 'I
desire mercy and not sacrifice.' For I did not come to
call the righteous, but sinners, to repentance."

MATTHEW 9:10-13

Tax Collectors and Other Sinners

Picture a long, low table with Jesus, His disciples, some tax collectors, and various other sinners reclining on every side. All were enjoying the lavish meal, and the flowing conversation was punctuated by jovial laughter. A good time was being had by all—except the Pharisees. Standing along one of the walls, arms crossed in judgment, they could not believe that Jesus was eating with *those* people, those tax collectors and sinners. Jesus calmly explained: "Those who are well have no need of a physician. . . . I did not come to call the righteous, but sinners, to repentance."

Jesus called the men—as He calls people today—to repent of their sins, receive God's forgiveness, turn away from those sins, and choose a Spirit-led life that will please and honor God.

We all need forgiveness—and we all can count on Jesus to grant forgiveness when we confess our sins.

60

HOPELESS?

*Then one of the twelve, called Judas Iscariot, went
to the chief priests and said, "What are you willing
to give me if I deliver [Jesus] to you?" And they
counted out to him thirty pieces of silver. So from that
time he sought opportunity to betray Him. . . .*

*[Jesus] answered and said, "He who dipped his hand
with Me in the dish will betray Me. . . . Woe to that man
by whom the Son of Man is betrayed! It would have
been good for that man if he had not been born."*

*Then Judas, who was betraying Him,
answered and said, "Rabbi, is it I?"*

He said to him, "You have said it."
MATTHEW 26:14-16, 23-25

Judas Iscariot

What do Judas's actions say about where he was placing his hope for this life—and the next? Clearly, he wasn't placing his hope in Jesus.

Although Judas—like the rest of the Twelve—had seen Jesus' love and compassion, Judas didn't buy into the Lord's program. Also like the other disciples, Judas had seen Jesus' miraculous healings as well as His power when He calmed the raging sea and walked through the crowd that wanted to kill Him. Yet Judas did not get on board. (Bible scholars have long speculated about whether we'll see Judas in heaven.)

Apparently Judas Iscariot didn't fully grasp Jesus' mission on this earth and was perhaps more interested in advancing himself rather than being part of Jesus' program. So Judas betrayed Jesus with a kiss, realized his terrible mistake, and hanged himself. Without Jesus, Judas was without hope. With Jesus, however, we are never without hope.

61

THE HOPE OF ANSWERED PRAYER

*[Peter] came to the house of Mary, the mother of John whose
surname was Mark, where many were gathered together
praying. And as Peter knocked at the door of the gate, a
girl named Rhoda came to answer. When she recognized
Peter's voice, because of her gladness she did not open the
gate, but ran in and announced that Peter stood before the
gate. But they said to her, "You are beside yourself!" Yet she
kept insisting that it was so. So they said, "It is his angel."*

*Now Peter continued knocking; and when they opened the
door and saw him, they were astonished. But motioning
to them with his hand to keep silent, he declared to them
how the Lord had brought him out of the prison.*

ACTS 12:12–17

Rhoda

Peter had had quite the night. Imprisoned, chained to two soldiers with two others standing guard at the door, Peter had been awakened by an angel who proceeded to lead him out of the prison.

At the same time, the church had gathered and asked God to have mercy on their imprisoned leader. Despite their earnest prayers, Peter's morning execution seemed inevitable.

A knock on the door interrupted their prayers. Recognizing Peter's voice when she went to answer it, Rhoda immediately ran to tell the people that God had delivered Peter. (When the knocking continued, they did go back to answer the door.)

Prayer is powerful! God hears and answers all our prayers—a truth that gives us hope. Just as the Lord answered prayers for Peter's life to be spared, He will answer your prayers with yes, no, or "Wait," whichever answer is best for you.

62

DEVOTION TO GOD

Six days before the Passover, Jesus came to Bethany. . . .
There they made Him a supper; and Martha served, but
Lazarus was one of those who sat at the table with Him.
Then Mary took a pound of very costly oil of spikenard,
anointed the feet of Jesus, and wiped His feet with her hair.
And the house was filled with the fragrance of the oil.

But one of His disciples, Judas Iscariot, Simon's son, who
would betray Him, said, "Why was this fragrant oil not
sold for three hundred denarii and given to the poor?" . . .

But Jesus said, "Let her alone; she has kept this for
the day of My burial. For the poor you have with
you always, but Me you do not have always."
JOHN 12:1–5, 7–8

Mary of Bethany

Consider snapshots we have of Mary of Bethany. In Luke 10:38–42, Mary was at the feet of Jesus, listening to His teaching. In John 11:32, grief-stricken Mary's words reveal her faith: "Lord, if You had been here, my brother would not have died." And in today's passage, Mary anointed the feet of Jesus.

We see in Mary a heart of devotion and a deep love for God and His truth. Hers was a humble, grateful, and generous love. She seemed unafraid of what people would think or what it would cost her as she lived out her love for Jesus.

When, in our devotion, we regularly go to the Lord in prayer, the Holy Spirit grows our love for God and His Word. He also provides us with the comfort and hope we need for this journey of life.

What, if anything, keeps you from sitting at the Lord's feet?

63

TRUSTING GOD EVEN WHEN . . .

Though the fig tree may not blossom,
Nor fruit be on the vines;
Though the labor of the olive may fail,
And the fields yield no food;
Though the flock may be cut off from the fold,
And there be no herd in the stalls—
Yet I will rejoice in the LORD,
I will joy in the God of my salvation.
HABAKKUK 3:17-18

Habakkuk

As followers of Jesus, we generally trust God to do what He promises to do—to protect us, provide for us, heal us, bless us. The real battle of faith comes when He doesn't come through with what we trusted Him to do. When God seems to ignore our request, what will we do? Continue to rely on Him despite our disappointment? Or turn away from Him and find our own path?

The prophet Habakkuk demonstrated the essence of true faith: continuing to trust and hope in the Lord's wisdom and faithfulness even when He seems inactive or—worse—uncaring. In difficult times, faith becomes a matter of the will, of deliberately choosing allegiance to the Lord regardless of the circumstances and despite His silence.

Even when all our resources and reserves vanish, may we say along with Habakkuk, "Yet I will rejoice in the LORD."

64

OBEDIENCE WITHOUT COMPROMISE

"Though they go into captivity before their enemies,
From there I will command the sword,
And it shall slay them.
I will set My eyes on them for harm and not for good. . . .

"Behold, the eyes of the Lord GOD are on the sinful kingdom,
And I will destroy it from the face of the earth;
Yet I will not utterly destroy the house of Jacob,"
Says the LORD.

AMOS 9:4, 8

Amos

God called Amos to prophesy to the Northern Kingdom, and Amos obeyed. Without any hesitation, arguments, or complaints, Amos went where God told him and shared God's message.

But a relaxed contentment had settled over the nation, and the people didn't welcome Amos's warning. Still, he faithfully performed his assigned task, trusting God's guidance, relying on His strength, and holding on to hope.

How many of us have Amos's persevering spirit? How many of us boldly proclaim the truth of the Lord in this hostile world? How many of us absorb blows from the Enemy and then take the next obedient step of faith?

As we choose to "trust in the LORD with all [our] heart[,] . . . lean not on [our] own understanding," and acknowledge God in all we do, He will enable us to persevere in our faith, share the gospel, and continue to obey Him (Proverbs 3:5).

65

THE HOPE OF NEW LIFE

*The hand of the LORD came upon me and brought me
out in the Spirit of the LORD, and set me down in the
midst of the valley; and it was full of bones. . . .*

*[God] said to me, "Prophesy to the breath . . . 'Thus says
the Lord GOD: "Come from the four winds, O breath, and
breathe on these slain, that they may live."'" So I prophesied
as He commanded me, and breath came into them, and they
lived, and stood upon their feet, an exceedingly great army.*

EZEKIEL 37:1, 9–10

Ezekiel

I n Ezekiel's day, hope had become a rare commodity, and the prophet himself must have felt as useless as the piles of bones God had shown him in a vision. He knew only a miracle could change the situation. Then, as Ezekiel watched, a miracle took place. Where only dry bones had littered the landscape, the Lord added muscles, tendons, and tissue. And into those once-dead bones God breathed new life.

Maybe you feel dry, defeated, emotionally scattered, or completely spent. Perhaps you sit alone, watching a panorama of death—the death of relationships, of dreams, even of people you love—unfold. Choose hope, not despair. If the God of Ezekiel is your God, you know that dry bones can live again. By God's grace, they can live empowered by His Spirit and find hope in Jesus Christ. So trust in the Lord and rest in His faithfulness.

66

GRIEF AND HOPE

The word of the Lord came to me, saying, "Son of man, behold, I take away from you the desire of your eyes with one stroke; yet you shall neither mourn nor weep, nor shall your tears run down. Sigh in silence, make no mourning for the dead; bind your turban on your head, and put your sandals on your feet; do not cover your lips, and do not eat man's bread of sorrow."

So I spoke to the people in the morning, and at evening my wife died; and the next morning I did as I was commanded.
EZEKIEL 24:15-18

Ezekiel

The day after He said He would, God took away
Ezekiel's beloved wife.

Grief-stricken, Ezekiel mourned, but not as his
culture dictated. Instead, as God had instructed him,
Ezekiel mourned privately; in public, he shed no tears.
When the people asked about his odd behavior, the
prophet explained that his sadness at his wife's death
was an example for them because they would soon be
grieving Babylon's destruction of Jerusalem. Maybe that
loss would be so profound that no tears would come. Or
the people might realize they had brought this loss upon
themselves with their disobedience and rebellion—that
the conquest of Babylon was deserved—and tears should
not come.

Just as He asked Ezekiel, God may ask us to do hard
things. We put our hope in the truth that He will be with
us and that His purpose is always good.

67

OBEYING THE ONE IN WHOM
WE PUT OUR HOPE

[The people] came near and said to Jeremiah the prophet,
"Please . . . pray for us to the Lord your God . . . that
the Lord your God may show us the way in which
we should walk and the thing we should do."

Then Jeremiah the prophet said . . . "Indeed, I will pray to
the Lord your God . . . whatever the Lord answers you, I
will declare it to you. I will keep nothing back from you."

So they said to Jeremiah . . . "Whether it is pleasing or
displeasing, we will obey the voice of the Lord our God
to whom we send you, that it may be well with us."
JEREMIAH 42:1-6

Jeremiah

Obedience is the joyful living out of what we know to be true, right, and good. It is following the Lord moment by moment, saying and doing what Jesus would do if He were in our place, submitting to His desires, and putting our hope in Him.

A mature Christian's passion to obey God is evident in hungering to know God's Word, desiring to do what is right before the Lord, and seeking direction from Him.

God's people went to Jeremiah wanting the Lord to show them "the way in which we should walk." The prophet was undoubtedly pleased with their commitment to know God's will and follow it. After all, obedience is the ultimate expression of our worship and service. But sadly, the people who approached Jeremiah did not obey the Lord's unwelcome instructions (Jeremiah 43:7).

We glorify God by obeying the One in whom we put our hope.

68

HOPE FOR LIFE'S FIRES

In this you greatly rejoice, though now for a little while, if need be, you have been grieved by various trials, that the genuineness of your faith, being much more precious than gold that perishes, though it is tested by fire, may be found to praise, honor, and glory at the revelation of Jesus Christ.
1 PETER 1:6-7

Peter

"In the world you will have tribulation," said Jesus (John 16:33). Jesus didn't offer any exceptions in the fine print. Tribulation—pain, loss, grief, frustration, betrayal, unfairness, injustice, disease—is unavoidable.

A trial can last for years (Paul's thorn in his side [2 Corinthians 12:7–10]) or for a brief time (the days between Peter denying his association with Jesus and reestablishing his relationship with his Lord). However long trials last, they—like fire refining gold—refine our faith in Jesus, revealing its genuineness and its impurities.

Paul learned about the sufficiency of God's grace, and Peter experienced the redemptive grace of Jesus' forgiveness. May those examples help us remember that God is for us, not against us. Trials come, and He uses them to grow our faith and make us more like Jesus. He wants us to know Him as our only Source of salvation, power, blessing, and, yes, hope.

69

WHAT WONDROUS LOVE!

At the ninth hour Jesus cried out with a loud voice, saying,
"Eloi, Eloi, lama sabachthani?" which is translated,
"My God, My God, why have You forsaken Me?" . . .

Then the sun was darkened, and the veil of the temple
was torn in two. And when Jesus had cried out with a
loud voice, He said, "Father, 'into Your hands I commit
My spirit.'" Having said this, He breathed His last.
MARK 15:34; LUKE 23:45–46

God the Father and Jesus the Son

The Trinity—Father, Son, Holy Spirit—is an indescribable and rather mysterious fellowship characterized by unity and love. Jesus' words can sound like a riddle: ". . . that [believers] all may be one, as You, Father, are in Me, and I in You; that they also may be one in Us. . . . just as We are one" (John 17:21–22). Puzzling if not incomprehensible, that prayer offers important context for some of Jesus' words from the cross.

Consider the oneness of Father and Son throughout eternity past: the separation Jesus experienced as He took on our sin was wrenching for both parties, making the crucifixion a vivid picture of profound love. God gave His only Son to take the punishment for our sins, and Jesus yielded to God's will. In the resurrection, Jesus defeated sin and death, freeing us to live a life of hope and joy, now and for eternity.

What wondrous love!

70

THE PROMISE OF STRENGTH IN
THE FACE OF TEMPTATION

Blessed is the man who endures temptation; for when he has
been approved, he will receive the crown of life which the
Lord has promised to those who love Him. Let no one say
when he is tempted, "I am tempted by God"; for God cannot
be tempted by evil, nor does He Himself tempt anyone. But
each one is tempted when he is drawn away by his own desires
and enticed. Then, when desire has conceived, it gives birth
to sin; and sin, when it is full-grown, brings forth death.
JAMES 1:12-15

James

God is *never* behind the temptations we encounter. Instead, as James wrote, our own desires are their source:

- Do we need or just want to purchase that [fill in the blank] that may bust our budget this month?
- In light of its theme and rating, is that movie a wise choice?
- Is social media a good use of time when the result is envy, jealousy, and ingratitude for what you have?

So, what can we do to resist such temptations? Paul told us in 1 Corinthians 10:13: "No temptation has overtaken you except such as is common to man; but God is faithful, who will not allow you to be tempted beyond what you are able, but with the temptation will also make the way of escape, that you may be able to bear it." With trust and in hope, turn to God and find strength whenever you face temptation.

71

OFFERING THE HOPE OF
INTERCESSORY PRAYER

Is anyone among you sick? Let him call for the elders of the
church, and let them pray over him, anointing him with oil
in the name of the Lord. And the prayer of faith will save the
sick, and the Lord will raise him up. And if he has committed
sins, he will be forgiven. Confess your trespasses to one
another, and pray for one another, that you may be healed.
The effective, fervent prayer of a righteous man avails much.
JAMES 5:14-16

James

A ll of us have prayed for people without seeing results, and we've been discouraged. James, though, declared that the "fervent prayer of a righteous man avails much." The corollary to that is our prayer will not be effective if our heart is unrighteous, filled with bitterness, resentment, or anger instead of Jesus' righteousness, love, and grace. If our intercessory prayer is to be effective, we need to confess our sins, pray for one another, and receive God's forgiveness.

Once we are forgiven, our intercessory prayers can be the link between a person's needs and God's inexhaustible resources. We can ask the Lord to reveal to us the person's true needs and reveal to that person the greatness of His love.

So, keep on praying, whether or not results are evident immediately. Your mere presence with a hurting person is a tangible manifestation of God's love—and a gift of hope.

72

THE HOPE OF RESTORATION

The LORD said to [Job's friend], "My wrath is aroused against
you and your two friends, for you have not spoken of Me
what is right, as My servant Job has. Now therefore, take
for yourselves seven bulls and seven rams, go to My servant
Job, and offer up for yourselves a burnt offering; and My
servant Job shall pray for you. For I will accept him, lest
I deal with you according to your folly; because you have
not spoken of Me what is right, as My servant Job has."

So [the three friends] went and did as the LORD commanded
them; for the LORD had accepted Job. And the LORD
restored Job's losses when he prayed for his friends.
JOB 42:7-10

Job

Satan made sure that Job suffered greatly, and Job's human friends made the situation worse. Eliphaz, Bildad, and Zophar did well—until they opened their mouths. Their silent presence with Job after his crushing losses was comforting and helpful. When they spoke, their words were not truthful and therefore not helpful—as God let them know.

Job had been humbled first by his loss and then by questions God asked him that pointed finite Job to God's infinite greatness. Repenting of his pride, Job asked God's forgiveness, and afterward, as God had instructed, prayed for his friends. Then we read, "The Lord blessed the latter days of Job more than his beginning" (Job 42:12). More important than the material restoration, though, was Job's restored relationship with God.

We find hope in Job's story: God restores the years we feel like we've lost, "years that the swarming locust has eaten" (Joel 2:25).

73

HOPE ROOTED IN RELATIONSHIP

*God said, "Let Us make man in Our image, according to
Our likeness; let them have dominion over the fish of the
sea, over the birds of the air, and over the cattle, over all
the earth and over every creeping thing that creeps on
the earth." So God created man in His own image; in the
image of God He created him; male and female He created
them. Then God blessed them, and God said to them, "Be
fruitful and multiply; fill the earth and subdue it; have
dominion over the fish of the sea, over the birds of the air,
and over every living thing that moves on the earth."*

GENESIS 1:26-28

God

Arguably, the greatest human need is to know we are loved, and God meets that desire as no human being can.

Our God—Father, Son, and Holy Spirit—lives in relationship, and He created human beings so He could be in relationship with us too. God also wants us to be in relationship with one another. Experiencing God's love enables us to love others well, and our love for one another is a powerful witness to God in this dark and broken world.

What an amazing truth, that God wants a life-giving relationship with us as our Savior, Lord, Father, Friend! He desires fellowship with us and worship from us. He longs to use us to build His kingdom on earth, and He loves opportunities to bless us.

So, ever doubt you're loved? Look at the cross. Let hope rooted in God's love for you replace every bit of doubt.

74

DOING HARD THINGS

*Though I might be very bold in Christ to command you
what is fitting, yet for love's sake I rather appeal to you . . .
for my son Onesimus . . . who once was unprofitable
to you, but now is profitable to you and to me.*

*I am sending him back. You therefore receive him . . . whom
I wished to keep with me, that on your behalf he might
minister to me in my chains for the gospel. But without
your consent I wanted to do nothing, that your good deed
might not be by compulsion, as it were, but voluntary.*
PHILEMON VV. 8–14

Paul and Onesimus

Philemon, a friend of Paul and follower of Jesus, had a slave named Onesimus. When Onesimus ran away, he—by God's grace—met Paul and became a follower of Jesus as well as a support for the imprisoned apostle. Even though he wanted to keep Onesimus with him, so "he might minister to [Paul] in [his] chains for the gospel," Paul knew that the right thing to do was return the slave to his owner, which—as Paul explained in this letter to Philemon—he was doing reluctantly.

No doubt Onesimus was nervous, but he returned home out of respect for Paul and his own desire to obey the God he loved. Onesimus's willingness to return also demonstrated the hope he had in Jesus Christ that Philemon would warmly receive him, now a brother in Christ (v. 16). We don't know Philemon's response to Onesimus, but we can be certain that hope in God enables us to do the hard but right things.

75

SHARING OUR GOSPEL HOPE

God is light and in Him is no darkness at all. If we say that
we have fellowship with Him, and walk in darkness, we lie
and do not practice the truth. But if we walk in the light as
He is in the light, we have fellowship with one another, and
the blood of Jesus Christ His Son cleanses us from all sin.

If we say that we have no sin, we deceive ourselves,
and the truth is not in us. If we confess our sins,
He is faithful and just to forgive us our sins and
to cleanse us from all unrighteousness.
I JOHN 1:5-9

John

Have you ever found yourself sitting on the sidelines of God's kingdom work, discouraged by sin and shame? Perhaps feeling God can't use you because of a sin you haven't forgiven yourself for or because you're believing lies about yourself? Don't let your feelings overshadow the truth.

And this is the truth: God is big enough to forgive you, restore you, and—by the power of His Spirit in you—use you to restore others. John put it this way: "If we confess our sins, [God] is faithful and just to forgive us our sins and to cleanse us from all unrighteousness." May that truth encourage you to walk off the sidelines and into the game.

After all, God only has flawed human beings like you and me to share the gospel for Him—and clearly He's made that arrangement work. The church still exists after two thousand years!

76

HOPING IN JESUS' RETURN

"Behold, I am coming quickly, and My reward is with Me, to give to every one according to his work. I am the Alpha and the Omega, the Beginning and the End, the First and the Last." . . .

"I, Jesus, have sent My angel to testify to you these things in the churches. I am the Root and the Offspring of David, the Bright and Morning Star."

And the Spirit and the bride say, "Come!" And let him who hears say, "Come!" And let him who thirsts come. Whoever desires, let him take the water of life freely.
REVELATION 22:12-13, 16-17

Jesus the Suffering Servant

He was born to a young woman and placed in a manger. He was a carpenter by trade with no place He called home. And this supposed Messiah didn't free the Jewish people from Roman oppression, as they had hoped.

Instead, Jesus first came to this earth as a suffering Servant. He served by healing the crippled, the bleeding, the blind, the leper; by calming the storm and feeding the multitudes; by astounding people with His teaching and upsetting the religious establishment when He called out their spiritual pride and hypocrisy. As a result, Jesus was misunderstood, betrayed, falsely accused, lied about, tried in illegitimate hearings, flogged, and crucified.

Yet this suffering Servant will return as the risen, glorious, conquering King. No one except the Father knows when. But in Revelation 22:20, Jesus says, "I am coming quickly." And we—His bride, members of His church—say, "Come!"

77

LIVING WITH PURPOSE

Later [the risen Jesus] appeared to the eleven as they sat at the table. . . . And He said to them, "Go into all the world and preach the gospel to every creature. He who believes and is baptized will be saved; but he who does not believe will be condemned. And these signs will follow those who believe: In My name they will cast out demons; they will speak with new tongues; . . . they will lay hands on the sick, and they will recover."

MARK 16:14–18

Jesus Christ

We all want our lives to make a difference; we all want to live with purpose. In today's passage Jesus clearly stated our ultimate purpose: "Go into all the world and preach the gospel to every creature."

Our almighty God is "not willing that any should perish but that all should come to repentance" (2 Peter 3:9), and He uses us to call people to repentance and salvation. By God's grace and power, the gospel message—Jesus died for our sin, was buried, and rose again—opens eyes blind to that truth, restores those held captive by their sin, and revives people dead toward spiritual truth.

Always pray before you share your faith; always depend on the power of God. Remember, the greatest force on earth is love. As you explain the reason for your hope and share your Christian love, you'll be living out God's purpose for you.

78

PUTTING HOPE IN THE ROCK

OF MY SALVATION

In You, O Lord, I put my trust;
Let me never be put to shame. . . .
Be my strong refuge,
To which I may resort continually;
You have given the commandment to save me,
For You are my rock and my fortress.

Deliver me, O my God, out of the hand of the wicked,
Out of the hand of the unrighteous and cruel man.
For You are my hope, O Lord God;
You are my trust from my youth.
PSALM 71:1, 3-5

David

What recurring image or theme appears in Psalm 71? Hint: Did you notice the words *refuge, rock, fortress,* and *deliver*?

When in this life have you needed refuge—and you found it in God? When has your faith in Jesus been your rock during a storm? What sin, struggle, pain, or wrong path has God delivered you from?

We are not to keep to ourselves our experience of Jesus working in our lives and being there when we needed Him. In fact, our story is a very effective way to share the gospel. After all, who on this planet doesn't need a refuge to run to, a fortress for protection, or deliverance from something?

The more we place our trust in God and the more openly we tell others about our experience of His mercy and grace, the more opportunities we have to share our faith and our hope.

79

ABIDING IN THE VINE

"I am the true vine, and My Father is the vinedresser.
Every branch in Me that does not bear fruit He takes
away; and every branch that bears fruit He prunes, that
it may bear more fruit. . . . Abide in Me, and I in you.
As the branch cannot bear fruit of itself, unless it abides
in the vine, neither can you, unless you abide in Me.

"I am the vine, you are the branches. He who
abides in Me, and I in him, bears much fruit;
for without Me you can do nothing."
JOHN 15:1-2, 4-5

Jesus Christ

In Jesus' description of His relationship with His Father is an invitation to us: "Abide in Me." Doing so is crucial: only when we live in a close relationship with Jesus—depending on Him and indwelled by His Spirit—can we bear fruit for God's kingdom.

The metaphor of the vine makes this spiritual truth clear: a branch cut off from the vine will not produce fruit. Just as branches need to be attached to the life-giving vine, we need to live attached to Jesus, the Source of our life.

Also, our lives need pruning just as a grapevine does. Only with pruning will the fruit be good. When too many leaves are on a vine, too much energy that could go toward producing fruit must instead go toward keeping those leaves alive.

So what specifically will you do to more fully abide in Jesus and therefore bear more fruit?

80

LOVING WITH A RADICAL LOVE

"You have heard that it was said, 'You shall love your neighbor and hate your enemy.' But I say to you, love your enemies, bless those who curse you, do good to those who hate you, and pray for those who spitefully use you and persecute you. . . . For if you love those who love you, what reward have you? Do not even the tax collectors do the same? And if you greet your brethren only, what do you do more than others? Do not even the tax collectors do so?"

MATTHEW 5:43–44, 46–47

Jesus Christ

If ever talk is cheap, it's in our overuse of the word *love*. We love traveling, swimming, reading . . . golden retrievers, dark chocolate, rainy days . . . and God, our spouses, our kids. But Jesus doesn't call us to a superficial, talk-is-cheap love. He called His followers in His day and calls us today to a costly love, to love that acts, that loves the hard-to-love, and that loves our enemies. Our love is to be radically different from love the world offers.

Jesus gave these specifics:

- When someone offends you, forgive. Doing so will help you avoid bitterness.
- Seek to understand before you seek to be understood.
- Practice listening and trying to understand the offender's perspective.

God's Spirit within you will empower you to love, with words and actions, even people who wrong you. Choosing God's way of dealing with people who hurt us means loving with hope in the One who heals hearts.

81

KNOWING HOPE WHEN OUR WORLD IS ROCKED

God is our refuge and strength,
A very present help in trouble.
Therefore we will not fear,
Even though the earth be removed,
And though the mountains be carried
into the midst of the sea;
Though its waters roar and be troubled,
Though the mountains shake with its swelling. Selah . . .

The LORD of hosts is with us;
The God of Jacob is our refuge. Selah
PSALM 46:1-3, 7

The Psalmist

Think about a day when your world was so shaken that you weren't sure it would ever be right again. When we put our hope in God, our world can be rocked—and it will be—but we have no reason to fear because our faithful God is a refuge that never changes and can never be moved.

The better we know God, the more readily we will seek Him as our refuge. Consider this command from later in today's psalm: "Be still, and know that I am God" (Psalm 46:10). How often do we make time to listen to the Lord? Making regular—even daily—appointments with God will help us better know the God who wants us to know Him better.

As we remind ourselves of God's sovereignty, His absolute goodness, and His abiding love for us, we can know peace and find hope despite our shaken world.

82

SALT AND LIGHT AND HOPE

"You are the salt of the earth; but if the salt loses its flavor, how shall it be seasoned? It is then good for nothing but to be thrown out and trampled underfoot by men.

"You are the light of the world. A city that is set on a hill cannot be hidden. Nor do they light a lamp and put it under a basket, but on a lampstand, and it gives light to all who are in the house. Let your light so shine before men, that they may see your good works and glorify your Father in heaven."

MATTHEW 5:13-16

Jesus Christ

Why salt? Why light?

First, salt is a preservative: the presence and prayers of God's people help to spiritually preserve a culture. Salt makes us thirsty: spiritual salt makes people thirsty for spiritual water, for the gospel. And just as salt enhances the flavor of food, our presence can enhance the places God has us.

As for light, it causes plants to grow, and God's light causes His followers to grow spiritually. Just as light guides, protects, and reveals in the physical world, the light of God's truth, values, and commands guides our steps, protects us from sin, and reveals His love and our purpose.

Do people recognize God's light shining from within you? Does the way you live—talk, parent, work, be a neighbor, coach soccer, or whatever it is you do—stand in sharp contrast to the world's ways? Being salt and light means the hope of Jesus comes to life in us.

83

LEARNING TRUTH IN THE DARKNESS

*Be anxious for nothing, but in everything by prayer
and supplication, with thanksgiving, let your
requests be made known to God; and the peace of
God, which surpasses all understanding, will guard
your hearts and minds through Christ Jesus.*
PHILIPPIANS 4:6-7

Paul

It's been a long while, but I will never forget a very dark time in my life. I was struggling in my job, and my marriage was in trouble. I reached out to a group of prayer warriors at my church, and during our Bible study I noticed Philippians 4:6–7 as if for the first time. I realized that the apostle Paul was sharing a hard-earned lesson. I was learning from the wisest.

When I read about not worrying about anything and praying about everything, these verses lit a fire in my heart, and I began praying about everything in my life. I gave *all* my troubles and struggles to God—who alone has the power and the wisdom to take care of them—and I left all of it with Him.

To this day, believing that God always wants the best for me gives me peace and hope.

HOPE THAT DOES NOT DISAPPOINT

"We speak what We know and testify what We have seen, and you do not receive Our witness. If I have told you earthly things and you do not believe, how will you believe if I tell you heavenly things? No one has ascended to heaven but He who came down from heaven, that is, the Son of Man who is in heaven. And as Moses lifted up the serpent in the wilderness, even so must the Son of Man be lifted up, that whoever believes in Him should not perish but have eternal life. For God so loved the world that He gave His only begotten Son, that whoever believes in Him should not perish but have everlasting life. For God did not send His Son into the world to condemn the world, but that the world through Him might be saved."

JOHN 3:11-17

Nicodemus

Jesus spoke these words to Nicodemus, a wealthy, educated, and powerful Jewish leader who was well respected by his people and a descendant of Abraham. Despite those credentials—as Jesus explained to Nicodemus—"you must be born again" if you want to see the kingdom of God (John 3:7).

Jesus wanted Nicodemus to realize that his only hope for entering the kingdom of God was Jesus Christ. Christian tradition holds that Nicodemus became a follower of Jesus, was baptized by Peter and John, suffered persecution from hostile Jews, lost his membership in the Sanhedrin, and was forced to leave Jerusalem because of his faith.

The only hope for salvation—for entering God's kingdom, for eternal life—is believing that Jesus Christ is God's holy Son who died on the cross to pay for our sins and that He rose victorious over sin and death. This hope will never disappoint.

HOPE-BASED ACTION

*I arose in the night, I and a few men with me; I told
no one what my God had put in my heart to do at
Jerusalem. . . . I went up in the night by the valley, and
viewed the wall; then I . . . returned. And the officials did
not know where I had gone or what I had done. . . .*

*Then I said to them, "You see the distress that we are
in, how Jerusalem lies waste, and its gates are burned
with fire. Come and let us build the wall of Jerusalem,
that we may no longer be a reproach." And I told them
of the hand of my God which had been good upon me,
and also of the king's words that he had spoken to me.*

*So they said, "Let us rise up and build." Then
they set their hands to this good work.*

NEHEMIAH 2:12-18

Nehemiah

L earning that the Babylonians had destroyed the wall
surrounding the city of Jerusalem and burned its
gates, Nehemiah wept in agony over the city's plight. But
he responded with more than just tears. Going before the
God of all wisdom, Nehemiah fasted and prayed—and
we can learn from his example. When we reach points
of despondency, despair, or desperation, may we also go
before the Lord with prayer and fasting, trusting Him to
provide clear direction.

Soon after learning about the wall, Nehemiah was in
Jerusalem to lead the rebuilding effort. Three days after
arriving, Nehemiah did his midnight reconnaissance
mission (today's Scripture passage). Building began
shortly thereafter. The project was not without its hic-
cups, but the wall was completed.

Having initially gone to God in prayer, Nehemiah
put his trust and hope in the almighty Lord to bless the
undertaking with success. May we do the same.

86

SAVED BY GRACE

God, who is rich in mercy, because of His great love with which He loved us, even when we were dead in trespasses, made us alive together with Christ (by grace you have been saved). . . . By grace you have been saved through faith, and that not of yourselves; it is the gift of God, not of works, lest anyone should boast. For we are His workmanship, created in Christ Jesus for good works, which God prepared beforehand that we should walk in them.
EPHESIANS 2:4-5, 8-10

Paul

Educated by the renowned Jewish teacher Gamaliel, Paul thoroughly knew and meticulously practiced the religious laws that directed almost every aspect of a Jew's life. What a contrast between life according to Jewish law and the message of grace Paul preached after he met Jesus on the road to Damascus!

God freely grants salvation to all people who place their faith in Christ. In response to God's great gift of His Son to die on the cross for us, we praise Him for His goodness. We thank Him for His love, and we remember that He loves us not because of anything about us. God loves us because He *is* love. He is also our Creator, and we are His work of art. God created us in the image of Christ, and we are still a work in progress. A beloved work in progress—and it's all God's grace!

87

"THE TRUTH SHALL MAKE YOU FREE"

Jesus said to those Jews who believed Him, "If you abide in My word, you are My disciples indeed. And you shall know the truth, and the truth shall make you free."

They answered Him, "We are Abraham's descendants, and have never been in bondage to anyone. How can You say, 'You will be made free'?"

Jesus answered them, "Most assuredly, I say to you, whoever commits sin is a slave of sin. . . . If the Son makes you free, you shall be free indeed."

JOHN 8:31–34, 36

Jesus Christ

The physical distance between our head and our heart is about twelve inches. That distance seems much greater when we want spiritual head knowledge to become transformative heart knowledge.

We can *know* from passages like today's that Jesus makes us free from sin. *Experiencing* that freedom is quite another matter. Or what, for instance, can we do to connect our knowing intellectually that Jesus loves us and our knowing His love experientially?

We know from Scripture that we are saved by faith alone in Jesus Christ, and we continue to learn Scripture's truth throughout our lives. But determining whether we will live in the joy of our salvation is both our personal response to Jesus' commands and our choice to spend time with Him.

When we obey Him and make our relationship with Him our top priority, we know hope in His grace, and we experience His love. Head and heart connect.

88

REMINDING US OF HOPE

"The Helper, the Holy Spirit, whom the Father will send in My name, He will teach you all things, and bring to your remembrance all things that I said to you. Peace I leave with you, My peace I give to you; not as the world gives do I give to you. Let not your heart be troubled, neither let it be afraid."
JOHN 14:26–27

The Holy Spirit

When we recognize Jesus as our Savior and, deciding to walk with Him all our days, we name Him our Lord, God blesses us with the gift of the Holy Spirit. The Spirit is the Guide whom Jesus promised to send His followers after He returned to heaven.

Among His many gifts to us, the Holy Spirit blesses us with the gift of peace when personal circumstances, the news cycle, a medical diagnosis, and work stress give us no reason to feel at peace. The apostle Paul described this gift as "the peace of God, which surpasses all understanding, [that] will guard your hearts and minds through Christ Jesus" (Philippians 4:7). This peace is beyond our understanding because the heart of Christ Himself is its supernatural source. With this peace comes a sense of God's presence, often renewed strength, and always a reminder of the hope we have in Him.

89

"DO NOT WORRY"

"Do not worry about your life, what you will eat or what you will drink; nor about your body, what you will put on. Is not life more than food and the body more than clothing? Look at the birds of the air, for they neither sow nor reap nor gather into barns; yet your heavenly Father feeds them. Are you not of more value than they? . . .

"Do not worry, saying, 'What shall we eat?' or 'What shall we drink?' or 'What shall we wear?' . . . For your heavenly Father knows that you need all these things. But seek first the kingdom of God and His righteousness."

MATTHEW 6:25-26, 31-33

Jesus Christ

Our heavenly Father doesn't want us, His children, to be anxious or worried about anything. Jesus said so in His Sermon on the Mount: "Do not worry, saying, 'What shall we eat?' or 'What shall we drink?' or 'What shall we wear?'" Jesus' directive is simple to understand but not always easy to live.

All of us worry about the basic necessities to some degree or at some point in life. We find it easier to worry than to trust and hope: *Yes, God has always provided—but will He this time?* Our answer determines our anxiety level.

What might help reduce that anxiety? The apostle Peter called us to "[cast] all your care upon [Jesus], for He cares for you" (1 Peter 5:7). This casting is not gentle fly-fishing. It is forcefully throwing something down at Jesus' feet—and not picking it up.

OBEYING GOD

"My covenant is with you, and you shall be a father of many nations. . . . I will make you exceedingly fruitful. . . . I will establish My covenant between Me and you and your descendants after you. . . . I give to you and your descendants after you the land in which you are a stranger, all the land of Canaan, as an everlasting possession; and I will be their God."

GENESIS 17:4, 6-8

Abraham and God

In Genesis 12, God called Abraham to leave his homeland—and Abraham did exactly that. When God gave that instruction to this man of faith, He also made Abraham some remarkable promises. Although they did not come to pass as quickly as Abraham might have expected, he kept following God.

Followers of God obey Him, and our understanding of God's sovereignty helps us obey. Most of the time Abraham's life demonstrated his confidence that God would do what He had promised.

So what can we do to better follow Abraham's positive example? Paul gave us this strategy: "Faith comes by hearing, and hearing by the word of God" (Romans 10:17). Studying and meditating on God's Word will help us know Him better, trust Him more, and then more willingly obey and more consistently live out our hope in our good God.

We trust and obey; God does the rest.

91

A LESSON ON PRAYER

"Our Father in heaven,
Hallowed be Your name.
Your kingdom come.
Your will be done
On earth as it is in heaven.
Give us this day our daily bread.
And forgive us our debts,
As we forgive our debtors.
And do not lead us into temptation,
But deliver us from the evil one.
For Yours is the kingdom and the power
and the glory forever. Amen."

MATTHEW 6:9-13

Jesus Christ

"T each us to pray" was the disciples' request, and the Lord's Prayer was Jesus' response (Luke 11:1). We first—and appropriately—acknowledge God's holiness and sovereignty, and then we humbly bow to His plan for the world and for our lives: "Your will be done."

Next, we address our physical and spiritual needs: we need food and forgiveness as well as the ability to forgive others.

Then comes our request for the Almighty's help in resisting the temptations presented by the world, the flesh, and the devil. We need to access Holy Spirit strength even as we request God's protection. The prayer ends with praise for the One to whom we pray, the One whose kingdom, power, and glory will last forever. Not a magic formula, the Lord's Prayer models for us intimate communication with the God of the universe, in whom we place our hope for the present and the eternal future.

92

THE WHOLE ARMOR OF GOD

Be strong in the Lord and in the power of His might.
Put on the whole armor of God, that you may be
able to stand against the wiles of the devil. . . .

Stand therefore, having girded your waist with truth,
having put on the breastplate of righteousness, and
having shod your feet with the preparation of the gospel
of peace; above all, taking the shield of faith with which
you will be able to quench all the fiery darts of the
wicked one. And take the helmet of salvation, and the
sword of the Spirit, which is the word of God; praying
always with all prayer and supplication in the Spirit.
EPHESIANS 6:10-11, 14-18

Paul

Belt, breastplate, sandals, shield, helmet, and sword—the Roman soldier to whom Paul was probably chained as he dictated these words was wearing exactly those pieces of armor. May we do the same!

Truth, righteousness, the gospel, faith, salvation, God's Word—this is the divine version of a prepared soldier's armor. In it the Lord has provided all we need for our journey through the fallen world, right now under the control of the Evil One, "the prince of the power of the air" (Ephesians 2:2). We need to put on the whole armor of God if we are to stand against the darkness of this world and the Enemy's attacks.

Finally, the truth of God's Word reveals to us the righteousness we have in Jesus as well as the gospel message of salvation that calls us to believe, grows our faith, and sustains our hope.

93

JOY EVEN IN PRISON

*At midnight Paul and Silas were praying and singing hymns
to God, and the prisoners were listening to them. Suddenly
there was a great earthquake, so that the foundations of
the prison were shaken; and immediately all the doors were
opened and everyone's chains were loosed. And the keeper
of the prison, awaking from sleep and seeing the prison
doors open, supposing the prisoners had fled, drew his sword
and was about to kill himself. But Paul called with a loud
voice, saying, "Do yourself no harm, for we are all here."*
ACTS 16:25-28

Paul and Silas

Paul and Silas had been attacked by a mob, beaten by soldiers, thrown into stocks, and shoved into a dark, high-security prison cell. How did they react to their new surroundings and discouraging circumstances? With prayer and song! Only the Spirit of God can produce joy in His people when we are in prison, whether that prison is literal or metaphorical.

Despite their exhaustion, Paul and Silas did not sleep. They chose instead to focus on God, and as they did, He blessed them with strengthened faith and hope. As they sang, a violent earthquake shook the prison, freeing from their chains everyone inside.

Whatever imprisons you right now, you have a song to sing. Express your willingness to trust God with your circumstances, rejoice that no problem is beyond His power, and expect Him to shake your prison. Lift up your voice in hope-filled anticipation of that coming victory!

94

"THE RIGHTEOUSNESS OF GOD, THROUGH FAITH"

*The righteousness of God apart from the law is revealed . . .
even the righteousness of God, through faith in Jesus Christ,
to all and on all who believe. . . . For all have sinned and
fall short of the glory of God, being justified freely by His
grace through the redemption that is in Christ Jesus, whom
God set forth as a propitiation by His blood, through faith,
to demonstrate His righteousness . . . that He might be
just and the justifier of the one who has faith in Jesus.*

ROMANS 3:21-26

Paul

Paul once prided himself on being the Pharisee of Pharisees: he knew the law as thoroughly as any of his contemporaries did, maybe more so—and he meticulously obeyed that law!

Yet this same Paul wrote, "All have sinned and fall short of the glory of God." His encounter with Jesus gave Paul that proper understanding of righteousness: he realized that only Jesus' death-and-resurrection victory over sin made a sinner's righteousness possible.

I will always remember when I first experienced God's unconditional, overwhelming, life-giving love. I still marvel that He likes spending time with me: He likes me to talk to Him, He likes talking to me through His Word, and He loves me simply because He is love. This amazing God has—by His grace—forgiven me because I have accepted Jesus Christ as my Lord and Savior. I praise God that He offers forgiveness and righteousness to you—to everyone—as well!

95

GOD'S REDEMPTIVE GRACE

Having been justified by faith, we have peace with God through our Lord Jesus Christ, through whom also we have access by faith into this grace in which we stand, and rejoice in hope of the glory of God. And not only that, but we also glory in tribulations, knowing that tribulation produces perseverance; and perseverance, character; and character, hope. Now hope does not disappoint, because the love of God has been poured out in our hearts by the Holy Spirit who was given to us.
ROMANS 5:1-5

Paul

A classic Sunday-school definition of *grace* is "undeserved favor." No matter how hard we try, we can do nothing to earn God's grace. God gives us the gift of salvation, and He continues to pour His grace into our lives after we receive Jesus as our Savior.

Paul considered it a privilege and a grace to preach the gospel truth—the gospel hope—he set forth in today's passage. Referring to God's call on his life, Paul wrote, "To me, who am less than the least of all the saints, this grace was given, that I should preach among the Gentiles the unsearchable riches of Christ" (Ephesians 3:8).

As Paul also noted, by God's redemptive grace, even tribulations are not for naught. In His grace, God surrounds us with His goodness and wraps us in His loving care, increasing our love for Him, sustaining our faith, and growing our hope.

96

GOD'S STRENGTH FOR OUR WEAKNESS

Lest I should be exalted above measure by the abundance
of the revelations, a thorn in the flesh was given to me, a
messenger of Satan to buffet me. . . . I pleaded with the
Lord three times that it might depart from me. And He
said to me, "My grace is sufficient for you, for My strength
is made perfect in weakness." Therefore most gladly I will
rather boast in my infirmities, that the power of Christ
may rest upon me. Therefore I take pleasure in infirmities,
in reproaches, in needs, in persecutions, in distresses, for
Christ's sake. For when I am weak, then I am strong.

2 CORINTHIANS 12:7-10

Paul

As a young Jew, Paul studied the Torah diligently, worked hard to keep that Law, and gained people's respect. Pride comes easily in such circumstances.

Once face-to-face with Jesus, though, Paul was forever changed. Then, as if that One-on-one with the Lord weren't awesome enough, Paul experienced an "abundance of . . . revelations" that might fuel his pride. God gave him spiritual insight that fulfilled his understanding of Jewish history and law.

To keep him a humble servant, the apostle wrote, God allowed—and didn't remove—a "thorn in the flesh." The unidentified infirmity proved a severe trial, humbling Paul, reminding him of his human weakness, and teaching him about strength in God. When our limitations prompt us to rely on God, we experience His strength for whatever we're facing. When we acknowledge our weakness, we—like Paul—can receive God's strength and, with it, hope for dealing with whatever life holds.

97

BE AN ENCOURAGER

*[We] sent Timothy, our brother and minister of God, and
our fellow laborer in the gospel of Christ, to establish you
and encourage you concerning your faith, that no one should
be shaken by these afflictions. . . . When I could no longer
endure it, I sent to know your faith, lest by some means the
tempter had tempted you, and our labor might be in vain.*

I THESSALONIANS 3:2–3, 5

Paul

———————————

A pastor at heart, Paul was concerned about the Thessalonian church he had founded: how was the people's faith in God holding up in this time of persecution? Paul sent Timothy to find out—and Paul rejoiced at the good report that Timothy brought back. Despite his own affliction and distress, Paul was "comforted concerning [the Thessalonians] by [their] faith" (1 Thessalonians 3:7).

Paul sent Timothy to encourage the Thessalonians, but then he returned with a report that encouraged Paul. Think about times when God has sent encouragement to you—and when He has used you to encourage others. Sometimes a single word, a soft smile, or a squeeze of a hand offers more encouragement than we realize.

Encouragement is always a blessing, but especially when the season is dark, the pain is suffocating, the road ahead is murky, and God seems far away. Who will you encourage today?

98

WAITING ON THE LORD

Oh, that You would rend the heavens!
That You would come down!
That the mountains might shake at Your presence . . .
To make Your name known to Your adversaries,
That the nations may tremble at Your presence! . . .
For since the beginning of the world
Men have not heard nor perceived by the ear,
Nor has the eye seen any God besides You,
Who acts for the one who waits for Him.
ISAIAH 64:1-2, 4

Isaiah

No one likes to wait, and apparently that has been the case for millennia. As Isaiah's cry for help reveals, the people of God wanted Him to save them right away. After all, He had acted on their behalf in the past.

Waiting doesn't come naturally to us human beings. In our hurry-up world, waiting can cause us to lose our temper, our good sense, and our control over our tongues more frequently than we care to admit. We want what we want right now. Yet the Word of God teaches that we learn some of life's greatest lessons while we wait.

Life's waiting rooms tend to be demanding classrooms, but God is with us when we wait on Him to act, to guide, or to make His presence with us known. God never wastes our times of waiting, and we can trust that He is at work in good but unseen ways.

99

"BLESSED ARE . . ."

"Blessed are the poor in spirit. . . .
Blessed are those who mourn. . . .
Blessed are the meek. . . .
Blessed are those who hunger and thirst for righteousness. . . .
Blessed are the merciful. . . .
Blessed are the pure in heart. . . .
Blessed are the peacemakers. . . .
Blessed are those who are persecuted for righteousness' sake."
MATTHEW 5:3-10

Jesus Christ

Our Lord came to this earth with teachings that were countercultural then, and they remain so today: "The last will be first" (Matthew 20:16); "Love your enemies" (Luke 6:27); turn the other cheek (Luke 6:29); and, yes, the Beatitudes. Take a moment to open your Bible to the Sermon on the Mount and read the second part of each beatitude.

When we choose to follow Jesus—when we choose to live in His countercultural, kingdom-of-God way—He blesses us in many ways. The Beatitudes speak of such gifts as comfort, righteousness, mercy, the ability to see God, adoption as His children, and a place in the kingdom of heaven.

The Beatitudes also reveal the results of the Holy Spirit's work in us to make us different from the world. May those differences make us winsome witnesses to our Lord, ready to share gospel hope and gospel love.

100

LOVE, HOPE, JOY, AND PEACE

*Now may the God of hope fill you with all joy
and peace in believing, that you may abound
in hope by the power of the Holy Spirit.*
ROMANS 15:13

Paul

———————————————

A Christian's life is to be characterized by love, hope, joy, and peace. That happens as we walk closely with Jesus, as the Holy Spirit makes us more like Jesus, and as we receive the hope, joy, and peace God offers.

First, blessing us with His sovereign and unconditional love, we find in God hope, joy, and peace whatever the circumstances, heartache, and worries of life. The promise of eternity with Him also fuels hope, joy, and peace.

Whether Paul was serving or suffering for Christ (2 Corinthians 11:23–27)—and he did both—he knew hope, joy, and peace. We can too, because God, our heavenly Father, is all-good, all-wise, and all-powerful. May we therefore make time to be with Him each day so He may "fill [us] with all joy and peace in believing, that [we] may abound in hope by the power of the Holy Spirit."

And all God's people said, "Amen!"

ABOUT THE AUTHOR

Jack Countryman is the founder of JCountryman gift books, a division of Thomas Nelson, and is the recipient of the Evangelical Christian Publishers Association's Jordan Lifetime Achievement Award. Over the past thirty years, he has developed bestselling gift books such as *God's Promises for Your Every Need*, *God's Promises for Men*, *God's Promises for Women*, *God Listens*, and *The Red Letter Words of Jesus*. Countryman's books have sold more than 27 million units. His graduation books alone have sold more than 1.6 million units.